Wajeeha Bilal is a writer with a passion for awareness, life, and books. She writes to inspire and awaken the readers through mindful awareness. She is the author of *The Beautiful Present* and the writer of her blog, *A Happy Awakening*. Having a master's degree in literature and exploring the different realms of literary writings, she has found her calling in the genre of self-realization, actualization, and awakening.

The credit for the completion of this book goes to the Higher Power, The Almighty, for guiding me through every lesson of my life.

Wajeeha Bilal

THE CONSCIOUS EGO

AUSTIN MACAULEY PUBLISHERS™
LONDON • CAMBRIDGE • NEW YORK • SHARJAH

Copyright © Wajeeha Bilal (2020)

The right of **Wajeeha Bilal** to be identified as author of this work has been asserted by her in accordance with Federal Law No. (7) of UAE, Year 2002, Concerning Copyrights and Neighboring Rights.

All rights reserved. No part of this publication may be reproduced, stored in a retrieval system, or transmitted in any form or by any means, electronic, mechanical, photocopying, recording, or otherwise, without the prior permission of the publishers.

Any person who commits any unauthorized act in relation to this publication may be liable to legal prosecution and civil claims for damages.

The age category suitable for the books' contents has been classified and defined in accordance to the Age Classification System issued by the National Media Council.

ISBN – 9789948356158 – (Paperback)
ISBN – 9789948356141 – (E-Book)

Application Number: MC-10-01-7521972
Age Classification: E

Printer Name: iPrint Global Ltd
Printer Address: Witchford, England

First Published (2020)
AUSTIN MACAULEY PUBLISHERS FZE
Sharjah Publishing City
P.O Box [519201]
Sharjah, UAE
www.austinmacauley.ae
+971 655 95 202

To my husband, Bilal, for his continuous support and contribution in helping me become a better writer.

Chapter 1

He did not raise his voice, but his words seemed strong enough to make an impact. He walked towards the window, with his hands knotted in a clamp behind his back. Strong and stressful without any amusement, she was bound to pay heed to this serious aristocrat.

"Life of deception and conceit is not what I will accept from you," he said sternly, looking outside the window.

"I am not asking you to lie, I don't believe in living like that too," she claimed, as she sat down on the far end of the couch. "But it is for the best and no one will end up getting hurt."

"I don't agree. You are letting yourself get hurt. You are ready to live a life depriving yourself and our child of my love. I will stay here and be a part of this family, no matter what you say." He was still facing the window and the room was heating up with the seriousness of their argument.

"You will have to let this go and go on with your life." She grabbed a paper from the side-table and started folding it into some shape. "It is for the best if we leave each other and never look back to what we had as a couple. Life is easier that way. I have my father to look after, and a child to raise. I can do it better without making things complicated for us." She started turning the paper into a small bird. It was her habit to make origami whenever she was nervous.

"Linda wants to get back and make things work again, but I need to ask you one time before going away, that is this really what you want?" The man softened his eyes and stared at her fragile hands that were busy making the origami.

"This is what is best for all of us, since I cannot be with you and we were never supposed to be together. We have separate lives. That is how it was always meant to be." She pressed the front of the paper with her nails and turned it into a sharp beak.

I got up from my bed to hear what was going on in the sitting room. I never entered without my mother's permission because I was always scared to be a part of something my mother didn't want me to know. So, I peeked through the corridor and saw a broad back facing the window with his hands behind his back and his little finger twitching with pace.

It was a small living room with a side partition that overlooked a small kitchen. It was an early summer morning and the sun was pleasantly warming up the room.

In fear of making any sound, I had left my shoes in my room. I slowly came closer in the hope of eavesdropping on my mother. My mother was sitting on the sofa-corner with her back towards me and her head was focused down.

"I am scared for you, how can you manage things at your own, I am ready to face the music and tell everyone about us if you let me," the man came closer and sat on the sofa next to my mom. She was still busy working on the origami. "Linda had chosen to leave me before I met you. She knows that, you just have to agree, and I will make our lives work together." He was looking at her fragile hands, the sun rays were hitting against his face, and I narrowed my eyes to get a better glimpse of who this man was.

"I have to let it work for me without making it complicated. My father is not well, and I must take care of him too. Besides, we have told Meryl and others here that the man I married had passed away a year after our marriage." She paused as the paper bird in her hand received a soft drop of tear. Her voice got shaky and she shook her head, "Also, so many years have passed, and the lie has made life better for me in many ways."

"I have been coming to you during all those years; you have to let me be a part of our family," the heat of the arguments had never worried him, but it was this cold aloofness that had threatened to engulf their relationship over all those years. "I cannot stop being a part of your life, but I am afraid if I go now, I may not return. Yet I promise you this, I will find a way to always be there for you and

Meryl, no matter the consequences." He stretched his hand to hold hers.

"I would rather have you go away and never speak of us as your family again. Meryl is turning nine and I do not want to complicate the things that have been going well for us." My mother took her hand and got another paper from the side table to make another origami shape.

"Loving you and Meryl comes naturally to me, just as making an origami out of paper comes to you." He looked straight and his voice was getting cold, "You have let your ego come in between us."

"You let your ego be the decisive factor when you could have declared your love for us nine years ago." My mother snapped, getting louder with her high-pitched voice. "But you were committed to your job and success. You chose your career and I can never get that time back. You could never make up for that and now I don't want to get back with you."

"I have tried to make amends for that over the last six years. You have to let it go now," his voice now had a stern intensity.

My mother stopped the movement with her hands and placed the pieces of paper on the table by her side. "I will tell you what; I will stop making origami and you will stop thinking about us."

"That is ridiculous. I can never stop thinking about you, just as you can never stop working on your origami." The man smiled at her to break the tension, but their egos seemed to strengthen with every sentence.

"I will prove it to you."

"You are making a big mistake."

"I will accept the blame."

"I am not blaming you."

"You are not liberating me either."

There seemed to be no end to this debate. I stood there with tapered, staring eyes, trying to figure out who the man was. I resisted blinking so that I could make out of his face through the sun rays. I moved closer without making any sound, the air around me was so calm that I could hear my own breathing. My teeth were getting tighter on my lower lip and my body was as still as ever, unblinking against my own movement. I felt a sudden jolt on my shoulder, my heart was pounding fit to burst, and my hands turned to fists. The grasp on my shoulder got tighter as I slowly turned around. My heart was throbbing through my temples and my eyes got wider, as I saw a huge man with a yellow masked face. He raised his other hand and my eyes opened like two flashlight beams.

I woke up to a cold and dark room. I tried to widen my eyes, my lashes faintly batting against the lids. My nightmares had the same yellow masked man appearing into my childhood memories. Instead of screaming, I stood still and stared at him, till I was drowned in cold, dead fear. I was trembling, my heart pounding against my chest, the remnants of the nightmare still clung to my mind. The room was still, and I could hear my own breathing. I gave out a loud cry as the alarm on my mobile threatened to take my life with its frightening sound, and I buried my face into the blanket. I swallowed and took the courage to press the silent button. I looked around and my eyes could pierce through the darkness and see the paintings on the wall.

Aside from my noisy breath, there was no one around, I assured myself that it was just a bad dream and I had to get back to the reality. I got up and made my bed, ready to start the day, my job did not permit me being late even on the weekends.

The bed was centered with white sheets and the white walls and curtains made the room brighter than an ordinary one. On the other side of the room was a small lounge with a reading corner. I had placed some of my paintings on the wall to make this hotel room more familiar. Where ever I moved; I would always make it my home. On the cabins near the fridge, I had placed a few of my kitchen tools and fresh produce. My mornings usually started with a few stretches and exercises, after which I was ready to go and win my day.

As I poured myself a fresh smoothie, the sun rays started to pour into my room. The room began to light up and I was glad that it was going to be a sunny day. Life in Paris around March comes as a relief after months of long, cold, and dark days. It may not be the livid sonata of blooms and spinning pollen that April and May frequently bring, but you can expect something like a mild thaw at work during this time of year. Although spring is on its way, March is generally still quite chilly, with lows, but this is the period when the French start to get back their *joie de vivre* and enthusiasm, and the city starts to feel livelier after a few sleepy months.

My hotel had a great service and location. One of the good things about U.N. jobs is that the organization takes good care of the people they have hired. As I always would say, the minds and bodies that are fed well execute their best.

After winters, I would usually dye my hair to a light auburn; not evenly, but in streaks, leaving warm browns in-between. It went well against my honey-toned skin. But my workdays were not the times to be self-conscious, I tied my hair up behind my head and in its messiness, it was even more suited to my outfit.

As a young girl, I had hardly bothered with make-up, since youth had made me attractive enough. Now that I had my toes in my third decade, things did not have to be so difficult like some women made it for them, who never leave the house without a full face-on. I did not want a mask on my aging that made me feel safe or without which I felt naked. There has never been any confidence in any tube or a beauty recipe in a bottle, it's just an illusionary ego in a palette.

Youth was not an illusion that I wanted to cling on to. I felt life from within. I was my own girl, robust, and real. The tailored suit of deep blue, revealing a lax white blouse at the neck of the jacket, was in the best of my tastes. Sliding into my stilettos, I headed towards the door.

There was that sensation in my stomach again, a soft mixture between queasiness and electric pricks. My head had begun to buzz, and my heartrate increased as I picked up my files that had the name SUNs stamped in bold. During my master's program in Peace Studies and International Relations at the University of Toronto, I worked with an African NGO, where I analyzed their arbitration efforts between ethnic communities, as well as their human rights work and capacity-edifice measures for stone excavation workers.

Experiencing the work of an NGO on a local level made me want to find out about the impact and scope of international organizations on the intergovernmental level. Having worked as one of the project managers of the National Model United Nations workshop at my university, I decided to apply for a position at U.N. Headquarters with the Carlo-Schmid Program (CSP).

The U.N. Peace building Support Office (PBSO) supports the Peace building Commission (PBC) with strategic advice and policy guidance. My position was with the Peace Building Commission Support Branch. I supported the work of the PBC Organizational Committee, which convened thematic meetings to address peace building challenges. Moreover, I supported all four peace building officers in their work with the six country configurations in doing research and drafting background analysis, taking points and summaries of the meetings. One of my favorite projects was the support for the drafting of the PBC against terrorism.

After that project, I was selected to be a part of the secret U.N. service for counteracting terrorism. We call them the SUNs in our private meetings. It is not an interrogative secret service with agents, but it is a private department working with and under the U.N. to deal with terrorism on a local level, where the agents act through peace. Apparently, we are professors of different subjects from different universities, collectively working as U.N. Volunteers but at the same time, we work secretly under SUNs, to identify and report any terrorist activities. SUNs is a recent development of the PBC, in collaboration with the FBI.

Peace, we believe, is not merely the absence of violence, but a will to initiate positive change from within, and a clear commitment to working with the people of different origin. I did research on specific aspects regarding the countries on the PBC agenda or crosscutting issues such as assisting the peace building officers with the preparations or follow-ups of the PBC meetings. I very much enjoyed learning about the relationship between the U.N. Secretariat and the Member States' missions and the specific workings of different processes. The possibility of being creative and thinking outside of the box in order to adapt to the changing situations on the ground was one of my favorite things of working with PBSO.

Work lied ahead and I placed everything in my work bag. It had been a week since I joined my team here, but heading to work always made me feel a bit nauseous, with the hopes that I would be at my best. By the time I would be at my work, my mind would be pumped with anxiety.

It was a sunlit day of early spring and the sky held a soft, blue glow. It was my first time in Paris, and I was beginning to fall in love with the city. There was no best neighborhood and no downtowns, since Paris's best things were spread out around the city center. The central area of the city had safe and walkable neighborhoods. It is one of the easiest cities to get around, even for first-timers, and most of the city is walkable or connected by a metro system. I mostly walked to places as that made it easier for me to get to know the city. We all lived in one hotel, but avoided meeting there or interacting. Every day, we would meet in a different café on the 11th arrondissement, to keep our meetings casual. Located in the lively 11th arrondissement of Paris, just east of the city center, and not too far from the Bastille, Passager Cafe could be found on the corner of a small side street, Passage de la Bonne Graine, and the larger Avenue Ledru-Rollin.

French for passenger, Passager itself felt more like a passageway, with a back set of doors leading out of the cafe onto Passage Josset. Open since 2016, the cafe was already a neighborhood fixture, in large part due to its warm, relaxed atmosphere. One barista described the cafe as "informal and comfortable, where you can do what you wish." When I arrived at the beautiful café, two guys were already waiting at the corner table for our meeting. Today was our second meeting since I came to Paris, but Chris and Jean had been friends before. Chris had travelled to France before and been in touch with Jean.

"Bonjour monsieur, what a lovely day." I greeted them both.

"Hey, Bonjour, your French accent is getting better," said Chris. He was a broad man with an average height and tanned skin. Chris Adams was an American, he was my supervisor when I was doing my internship in the U.N. Peacebuilding Support Office (PBSO) at the U.N. Headquarters in New York.

"Bonjour," nodded Jean Andre with a slight grin. He was a tall, French man with a French origin. His shoulders hunched together like he was trying to disappear inside himself that made him seem shorter than his actual height. He looked like a shy version of Chris. If you didn't know them better, they would appear like brothers who had nothing in common, except their blonde hair. Jean was the local photographer and he was entrusted to be a kind of guide for us.

"You should try the latte here, they are exquisite," exclaimed Chris, raising his cup to me.

"I am more of a juice person, caffeine makes me dizzy." I sat down and placed my bag on the chair next to me.

"Bonjour," we all stood up to greet our team leader, Emre Miraç. Emre had worked as the United Nations Volunteer Program Officer (UNVPO) for a few years and traveled across many countries. He had the kind of face that stopped you in your tracks. His face was strong and defined with dark, brown hair. He was handsome from the depth of his eyes to the gentle expressions of his voice.

"Bonjour everyone." Emre greeted everyone with the most attractive smile I had ever seen on anyone. He was the kind of man that made you pause for a while and then think about what you had to say. "We are all here right on time." He was waiting to hear our voices so he could direct his voice to us.

Yes, one thing I forgot to mention that he was blind. His magnetic aura overpowered you in a way that you would forget that he could not see. Another reason was also his peculiar movement, he did not at all act or walk like someone who had no sight. For everything was accurately measured by his other senses, as he had told us on our first day here.

"Peace is not merely the absence of violence, but a will to initiate a positive change from within, and a clear commitment to working with the people of different origin." We all declared unanimously.

"Amen to that!" Chris raised his glass and we all smiled, "Would you like to get something before that?" asked Chris, trying to be friendlier.

"No, I am fine," replied Emre, looking straight at him, where no one could suspect that he was blind. "Last Thursday, we had discussed our new assignment 'The Eglise,' what are the updates on that, Jean?"

"I was able to get some pictures of the church, as I told them that I needed to publish these in the upcoming issue of 'Lire' and…" Jean took out some pictures and laid them on the table. "There is no entrance to their private chambers, the passage is from within the church," explained Jean, as he pointed to some of the pictures, "There aren't any entrances other than the front and the back door, but the inside of the church is even more complex than it looks." Jean handed us some pictures with the close ups of the church's interior. "There are no hidden doors or passages. In fact, the church and its chambers are open to the visitors the whole day and even after the sunset, anyone can feel free to pray, as long as they stay in the aisles and do not approach the nave."

We all got hold of some of the pictures, while Emre listened carefully.

"Apparently, there are no secret doors or entrances, as the interior is designed for the reason of prayers only, except for a small entrance at the back of the nave." Chris pointed to one of the pictures. "We went over these yesterday and came to realize that this was the chamber secluded for the pastors and ministry staff so no one else had access to it."

"There is a room at the back of the church for the office and maintenance staff that are also a few in number," added Jean, "So, the only people allowed to meet in these rooms are those working for the church."

"So that means, the people we are looking for are actually all those that work for the church," Emre backed their logics with one statement.

Chapter 2

"Immigration to France increased during the wars of liberation and decolonization in the 1950s and 1960s, especially in the free and unregulated entries of immigrants from Algeria," Jean explained, taking out some documents, "With the signing of the Evian Agreement, new arrivals included former French colonists' resident in Algeria, as well as Algerians who had sided with France."

"In July, 1974, the French government followed the lead of other European counterparts and officially ended its labor migration programs," continued Chris, "The legislation also included provisions for sanctions, affecting employers who hired illegal immigrants, a French policy innovation originally developed in the 1930s." Chris looked up from his laptop and rested his chin on his hands, "Guys, this continued in the '80s because I had a friend once who told me that she knew a lady whose mom migrated from Algeria to France and a French businessman who gave her a job and refuge, stayed in hiding till they all had to migrate to Canada and seek refuge there." Chris got serious and his eyes widened, whenever he took us off the topic to relate to something he knew personally, "The woman actually bears the child of the man she used to work for," he said slowly, trying to make an impact with his sad story while nodding along, making us feel worse for the immigrants.

"Nonetheless, immigration continued and diversified over the following decades," Jean continued, trying to complete his historical facts for our meeting. "After Charles Pasqua put forth the goal of 'zero immigration,' a group of Africans and Chinese who were unable to obtain residence permits – even though many had resided in France for several years and could not be legally deported – occupied a church in Paris," Jean was pointing to the pictures of the church again.

"These 'sans papiers' (people without legal documents) mobilized the support of over 10,000 people, who marched in Paris on their behalf." Chris gave some more facts relating to our story of 'The Eglise.' "The police broke up the demonstration, but similar acts of civil disobedience by the sans papiers and their supporters continued throughout the 1995 to 1997 period."

"So, these people have been suspected of being in touch with Al-Qaeda and ISIL, but there is no apparent proof." Emre tried to settle the research by giving us the details of what had been assigned to us, "After the 2015 Paris attacks, all the staff and pastors were put to question, and no evidence linked them to any of the terrorist attacks."

I was taking all the data down for the draft details that I had to submit to the headquarters. The details were necessary to keep the authenticity of the historical facts and to keep everyone on the same page. With the written drafts of the meeting, it was clear that the facts could not be distorted.

"Since then, the church has gained more popularity and its people continue to make an impact through their teachings, there is no distinction between any races as all the staff now comprises of those refugees. Their message is for all and everyone, of every color and race." Emre always had a smile on his face, even while talking about the most strenuous events. I had never seen a person more positive than him.

"Could they be deported on the suspicion charges of their connection and under the Pasqua law?" I asked, trying to get my facts straight.

"They were tried under those and after no proof, no action could be taken due to the huge impact they have on the masses." Emre looked right at me and I could never guess that he could not see. His eyes so precisely focused on my face. How could someone who was not able to see be so accurate in sensing where my face was, I thought to myself, as I took down more facts.

"I don't think anyone can do anything when these people have a strong standing with not only the locals, but also with the people of their own countries. Their message is of peace and for everyone." Jean added, "The church has expanded ever since and when we say people from other countries, we mean a lot of other races."

"That's what we are to do. Since they have an impact on a huge number of people, we have to be a part of the peace message and get into their roots. As peace makers, we must make sure that there are no secret services being done for encouraging violence within the country…" Emre had sensed someone approaching our table.

"Are you waiting for someone else to join you?" The waitress smiled at us with the eagerness of someone new to the job and asked if she could get us any drinks.

"One fresh orange juice," I smiled at her.

"One of your topnotch lattes," said Emre, smiling at her. It was astonishing how he could guess where her face might be, just after listening to her.

Chris and Jean both got a refill for their lattes. The waitress stood with what looked like a mini touchscreen computer and as we spoke, she nimbly tapped the screen to communicate the order straight to the kitchen and left.

"As peacemakers, our most precious weapon is our speech." Emre got back to briefing us after the waitress left. "We are armed with words and passion. People who have suffered or have seen their families suffer need to know that we not only understand their pain, but are ready to help them grow out of it. The miseries of the past cannot be accommodated through revenge, but their lives and their loved ones need a new beginning and a better ending. The magic of healing lies within every human being as long as they are ready to listen to the language of love." Emre paused, while we got our drinks.

Chris leaned forward and made his serious face, "Debate for us is verbal war and mastering our language to use it as a tool for peace is what will help us make a difference as peacemakers."

"Yeah man, you made it all clear now," Jean smirked at Chris.

"Your words should resonate with how your listener feels and the speech should come from the heart." Emre took out some files and laid them on the table. "Grab the files with your names on them. Understand your roles as peacemakers and most importantly, why you are here to help these people. We will be arranging for a meeting with the pastor and you will be updated soon for our next schedule. Remember that we are foreign professors from different universities here, with the mission to spread knowledge about International bonding. No one needs to know about our affiliation with the U.N. secret services targeting terrorism."

We all took our files and Jean started packing his pictures.

"I have to attend a photo gallery festival." Jean always seemed to be in a hurry. Photography was his passion and he was always busy with one event or another.

"Jean, you will be always ready at every sermon as our photographer." Emre then turned to Chris and me, "Chris will be the assistant lecturer who will lay the introduction for our lectures and Meryl is our consultant who will be following the lecture and taking queries for the next speaking session."

"Au revoir," Chris took his files, waved us a goodbye, and joined Jean on his way out.

"Mr. Emre," I said hesitatingly, "You can always feel free to assign me something more than just taking notes at the session. I mean, I volunteered for this job and I can do a lot more."

"Yes, I am sure you are capable of doing the best," Emre smiled at me, while getting up. He followed his way out and I slowly grabbed my files, putting them in my work bag. I felt like I should have been given something to speak for, so I would know for sure that I was making a difference in bringing peace to the world. That was the reason I had joined the U.N. I felt a bit let down. I took my bag and headed home.

I saw Emre wearing his sunglasses and headphones to get directions from his app. Since we were both headed in the same direction, I thought to join him. I didn't have the gut to ask him the last time, but I thought I would now. His enthusiasm for life interested me and now I really wanted to know how he was so good at sensing things, at precisely knowing if an object or a person was near him and how could he walk without his stick.

"You don't mind if I join you?" I asked him.

"Of course not, I love company." Emre took out one of the earpieces and started walking.

"I could guide you along, if you want, you can leave both the headphones off," I said, trying to be of help.

"Yes, you can guide me too, but I will keep my help with me," said Emre, walking slowly, listening to his directions and sensing for anything that might come his way. "You can tell me what you see along the way." Emre paused a little and looked towards me, "Are you heading to the hotel or do you have anything other planned for today?"

"I actually wanted to get some grocery too, but I can do that later, I would rather chat a little with you today. I mean, Chris and Jean have great company together, but don't you get a bit lonely? I know I do," I said, quickly trying to sound very friendly and I hoped that I was not offending my boss with anything.

"I guess then we can head towards the market that falls on the route, I can enjoy the local market tour instead of having everything through room service today." Emre spoke into his mobile to change the location on his app. I kept telling Emre about the people and places around us and he told me a bit of historical facts as we slowly moved on.

Characterized by laughter, joy, and the toasting of glasses, the 11th arrondissement is a hub of activity and cultural diversity that's not to be missed.

The 11th arrondissement had long been known as a lively melting pot, where happy locals and tourists alike sipped wine and shared great food with friends. The quartier's unrivalled pleasant atmosphere had earned it the desired reputation of the arrondissement, which best embodies the *joie de vivre* of the city.

From a historical perspective, the 11th is an area which represented change. It was here that Parisians began the French Revolution, with the storming of the Bastille on the 14th of July, 1789. Today, the Colonne de Juillet, the towering, golden, Corinthian statue honoring the Revolution of 1830, rests on the site of the old prison at Place de la Bastille. Just adjacent to the Colonne de Juillet was Opéra Bastille.

Vibrant, ethnically diverse, and undeniably trendy – that's the 11th arrondissement. Its boulevards and avenues span out from Place de la République towards the east, like Boulevard Voltaire and Avenue de la République, delineating this wedge of the city into its own distinct parts with their own character and atmosphere. Historically a blue-collar district, the 11th had evolved a great deal in recent years, due in part to the influx of young professionals seeking lower rents and an active nightlife. Over time, this gave way to a sort of gourmet renaissance, attracting younger chefs and inspiring envy in residents of the more expensive parts of town.

It took us about 15 minutes to reach the market. The 11th is also home to two of the biggest open-air markets in the city – Marché Bastille and Marché Popincourt. For many Parisians, these markets are part of a weekly ritual, Marché Bastille bustled with stalls burgeoning with fresh fruit and vegetables, meat, fish, flowers, souvenirs, clothes, and trinkets.

Emre told me to head towards Sabah. "It's one of my favorite shops in Paris," he told me.

"You have been here before?" I lent him my hand, as it got more crowded.

"Yes, but that was a long time ago." He held onto my arm but still relied on his own intuition. There were two stalls adjacent to the market. He got some Asian spices and dates.

Walking down the main street of the market, there was a phantasmagoria of places that line the rue d'Aligre, where vendors set up on the street and sold fruits, fresh vegetables, and big bundles of herbs. Since many of the vendors had similar fruits and vegetables, some would shout out to shoppers to buy, as they passed to get their attention. Instead of being afraid of people hollering at customers, as it's not something we're used to in the States, Emre told me to just smile as they were all friendly and that's just what they did. I bought some fresh produce and Emre's French was so perfect that people actually thought him to be a local there.

We also tried a cut-up pineapple and I smiled as Emre engaged with all the sellers, whether we bought something or not. "The French are pretty discerning shoppers, so if you're not interested in something, thank them, and move on," he told me.

Chapter 3

We separated just five minutes before reaching our hotel. Le Pavillon de la Reine, in the heart of Le Marais, both one of the most famous and most historical districts of Paris, the Pavillon de la Reine perpetuated an elegant atmosphere combined with discreet luxury to attract the most stylish globetrotters in the world, in their quest for a quiet and discreet place to relax.

The Pavillon de la Reine is embellished with its shady gardens and its distinctive façade.

In a 17th century building tucked away from the galleries and shops of the Place des Vosges, which was built in 1612 by King Henry IV of France. The hotel's name was a nod to the building's history, in honor of Queen Anne of Austria who once stayed in one of the wings. While the Place des Vosges was once the center of high society in Paris, today, Le Marais shines as one of Paris' most exciting quartiers – with Pavillon de la Reine at its heart.

It offers a universe with a subtle and contemporary charm and unexpected combinations of material, colors, and styles. Classic and superior rooms run small, but are enlivened by brightly patterned wallpaper, colorful throws, or wrought-iron window boxes filled with flowering plants. I could enjoy nature from my own room. I placed my bag and files on the couch and fixed myself some lunch. I was very hungry after a long walk.

I settled in my couch and looked outside the window. There is something about nature that soothes the senses. This calmness felt like a blanket that covered me from the cold anxieties of being at work. My eyes felt heavier and my mind drifted into a peaceful silence, when I felt someone's hand touching my forehead.

"Mom, what are you doing here?" I asked, looking up at her.

"Your friend is here with a surprise," she told me, while helping me get up. "Now hurry up, Meryl, and meet us downstairs."

"I will come with you, Mom," I said hesitatingly. My mother had this zest for life. Though my father had left us, she always faced life with a smile on her face. I sometimes felt that she pretended to make life happier for me but when embracing life and greeting everything and everyone, I was amazed at how someone who was disowned by my father, be so bright. She created the warmth in my life and I mostly followed her, for without her everything seemed incomplete. She had an internal happiness, one completely independent of the external world. She beamed like an eruption from within, instead of wearing a smile like an obligation, the way others did.

I followed her down and the room was suddenly lit with a roar of "Surprise," with my best friend, Samantha, holding a birthday banner. She had called a few of our college friends too. Samantha was our neighbor and my childhood friend. She was a few months older than me, but she was a very sweet girl who had a big heart for tolerating others, so maybe that is why she was kind of the only friend I had.

"Aww, happy birthday, my dear," my mom hugged me as she took me towards my friends. I didn't like celebrating birthdays so I forced a grin and said thanks in a way that they could guess I didn't like it. I wanted to smile but the corners of my mouth didn't twitch, maybe because I hardly smiled or laughed. I watched and read a lot of funny things but never relegated to anyone. I also did not hug – ever.

I sat on the chair they had placed with all the birthday decorations and my mom lighted up the candles on the cake, but their glow could not overpower the brightness on my mom's face. The room was surely lit up when Samantha's dad walked in, carrying a giant present for me. I smiled and received the huge gift. This smile was the happiest that I have ever been. Her dad was the best father that anyone could ever wish for. He never missed any of our school functions or any of our parties. He was there at every occasion, cheering us up, both me and Samantha. Now, he made sure not to miss my birthday. I wondered why life didn't bless me with a father like that. No wonder

Samantha stayed happy. There was no need for me to be happy when my father left me and didn't even care for any of the life's occasions. My mother looked at my stunned face and leaned down to kiss me.

"Now dear, it's your birthday and we are all here for you," she said, handing me the knife. "So, love what you have, and forget what you could have had," my mom whispered to me.

Everyone sang to me as I blew out the candles and cut the cake. Samantha blew the tooty-tooter in my ear, *"toot,"* the sound was getting annoying now. *"Toooot, tooot."* I woke up to the sound of beeping that wasn't a tooter but the mobile beeping on the side table. I listened, still focused on my memory. I moved slowly to awaken my body that seemed heavier. I rolled to my right side and slowly stretched my body, opening my eyes wider as I moved to pick up my mobile.

There were a few updates from our head office that demanded me to send the draft of today's meeting by tomorrow and had told us to schedule the conference after three days. We were also notified that Emre was required to go for a short official visit of about a week in the upcoming month. If any of our seminars fell during that week, then Chris would be conducting the main speaking event in Emre's absence. Emre would brief us about the details later.

I sat down to send the draft but found it hard to focus. I started thinking that why wouldn't they ask me to speak at the event or at least follow the proceedings. I spent some time writing details from my notes and before submitting it, I thought to give it a final reading. I looked outside and saw the daylight draining away. It was getting darker and cooler.

I slipped into my jumpsuit and wore my slip-ons as I headed out. It was surprising that the day that had promised of spring's arrival was now ready to betray that promise to the coldness of the night. I tugged my hands in my pockets and trudged towards the open park at a sedate pace, my mind focused on what I was here to do in my life. It was one of Paris' most beautiful squares, and the park was just a minute or two from our hotel. I looked for a bench and saw Emre sitting on the corner bench. I wanted to avoid him, but something forced me to go up to him and talk about the work.

I sat next to him; he didn't look at me, but seemed to have recognized my presence.

"This is a beautiful place to sit and enjoy, especially when one is down," he smiled, still looking straight. His gaze was focused on the sound of the water fountain. "What do you think, Meryl?"

"How do you know it's me?" I raised my eyebrows and asked him.

"People can easily be distinguished by the energy they put out through their feelings." This was the first time Emre had directly answered a question that was about his power to feel things accurately. He took a deep breath and sensed the air around, "Place des Vosges is well-known and loved with good reason. It has the distinction of being the oldest planned square in the city. Its example was followed throughout Europe." Emre seemed to know a lot about history. He could tell you about anything you asked him, and he would also tell you about the historical facts even if you didn't ask him. It was like an ice breaker for him. Most of the questions that were directed towards his personal life or qualities were mostly answered in a way where he would narrate about the historical facts for something or their present-day values. "It was commissioned by King Henry IV, and inaugurated in 1612 for the wedding of his son, Louis XIII," he pointed in the direction of a statue, in the middle of the square, mounted on horseback. "The square was unique at the time because the style of the building facades were designed to be uniform and harmonious, featuring all that gorgeous red brick."

He is a super genius, I thought to myself.

"The square was first called Place Royale, a place for the wealthy. Two of the houses on the square were for the king and queen (the two highest ones), although they were never used by royalty. The Marais still bears hints of its past royal inhabitants, like the street name 'Rue de Parc Royal,' not too far from Place des Vosges. A few other names occurred after the revolution, until the name, Place des Vosges, was settled on by Napoleon. He needed the country to pay taxes and renamed the square as recognition to the first department of France to pay the tax. Although royalty is long gone, purchasing a property on this square nowadays is some of the most expensive real estate in the city per square meter. But thankfully for us common folks, we can still enter the park for free and enjoy the serene setting." He smiled and turned towards me.

"Wow, you know everything. I mean, there was not a single thing even on our shopping tour that you did not know about." I wanted to ask him, but stayed quiet for I was already feeling down and looked straight.

"What are you thinking?" he asked me directly, sensing that I had stopped talking. "Is there some problem?"

"Nothing. I mean, I was expecting that I would at least be considered for speaking at our peace conferences or given a better role than just taking down notes." I was not hesitating anymore. "Is it because I am a woman, is it? I mean, why won't I be preferred for some senior roles? I am as qualified as Chris."

"Ah, since you mentioned his name. You see, here is someone who lives by learning about this city and working every second to know things that even the locals don't. And then there is another person who took the job of actually staying with the U.N. to get away from the family troubles, having good reason to stay away from the family at the same time might help in the peace process too." He passed a sly smile as I looked at him.

"You don't know anything about my family," I said quickly, still shocked at what he had said. I felt like he had judged me, or was he right? I mean, he made me think like I had not thought before.

"I am not saying I do, neither am I here to judge you, but you seem pretty upset," he said softly, making up for his statement.

I stayed quiet for I did feel like I had been judged. I was feeling a bit embarrassed now. This moment would become a memory that would sprout in my brain to torment me next time. With each moment getting colder, night was falling quicker than ever. His words had seemed colder than the wind that bit me right where it hurt. I wrapped my arms tighter around myself, pulling my jumper closer and tucking my chin downward into my pullover.

"I am sorry that you felt sad over that email," he said, softly still making up for the cold words. "If it would make you feel any better, is there anything I can help you with?" he asked, turning towards me again.

"I thought I could do a satisfying act in my life –" I spoke slowly.

"You don't have to feel compelled to explain anything to me. I am not here to judge anyone," he interrupted me. "We are all doing our jobs and what we think we are good at or makes us happy. It's just who we as humans are."

He had never explained anything so directly, I looked at him and asked him intently, "How do you do all this? How do you know everything so well?"

"We are all lucky to be born in this world of technology, we would be doing ourselves damage if we didn't polish ourselves with the latest techniques," he told me.

"I understand you work hard to learn but how do you know about people and their feelings or what they are thinking. You must have worked hard but I have never met any person utilizing a disability to this much advantage. I mean, you are better than all of us who can see." I let it all out. The things I had been meaning to ask him since I met him.

"There is more to life than all that you see or think." He simplified it for me, "This is a beautiful park and taking a walk here would make you feel better –"

"Please don't, please don't change the topic," I interrupted him. "Let me know how you do it all or how you taught yourself to do it. Maybe that can be something you can help me with. I mean, I am not saying tell me the whole story, but just simple steps or a bit of how you started learning to utilize your senses better." I was begging him for it now.

"It has a lot to do with feelings," he said, sensing that it was not easy to get out of it, "I will try to make it easy for you to understand this since you are keen, I will see what I can do to help," he got up to leave, slowly feeling his way back.

Night came like the enchantment of a sorceress, there was no clue of warmth left, nothing of the spring, or the pat of the defeated sun. The dark had robbed the night of its promising warmth that was assured by the declining sun.

Chapter 4

I crept into my bed after submitting my reports, I had always been an early sleeper, but I found it difficult to close my eyes. My thoughts raced from the conversation I had in the evening, to the work assignments, and random events from the past. I never wanted a job where sleeplessness was a casualty but here, I was lying in my bed and wondering how unfulfilling my life was.

Maybe I was lonely or unhappy because of my life's choices, I thought to myself, when suddenly I heard a knock on the door, and something being dropped at the bottom. It was so quiet I could hear someone placing something at the door. I quickly got out of my bed with a restless jerk and went to open the door. I found a parcel that had my name and room number on it. I looked out of the door towards left and right, but nobody was in sight. I went inside to open the yellow packing. I sat down on my couch and unwrapped the yellow layers, uncovering a huge red book that had the words, 'Feel the truth that is unseen,' carved in golden metal on it.

I pressed my fingers on top of those and closed my eyes while I moved my fingers slowly along those letters,

'FEEL

THE TRUTH

THAT IS UNSEEN'

I said out loud as I felt the letters on my fingertips. The metal words felt cold against the warm velvety red cover. I opened it to see what it was about, and it was like opening my laptop. The book was heavy and large with huge letters carved in metallic gold that could be felt with your hands. It contained large off-white papers that too were encrypted with the metallic gold letters. On the left corner, at the back of the cover was a small note that said; *'Discover the truth that you seek and uncover the reality that your sight ignores.'*

I turned to the main pages and started feeling the writing on the paper as I moved my fingers across it.

You are here right now and going through these words that were written just for you. You not only read them but feel them too. Your mind that is reading me silently has an amazing power to do extraordinary things while managing to keep you alive.

I paused a little, opened my eyes and looked at those words that seemed so real. It was like the book was talking to me with a silent language that only I could understand and feel. It felt astounding, so I closed my eyes again and moved on.

You are thinking right now about this book that you are reading, so feel the words and focus on how you can focus your mind on these words right now. You are thinking of something else too right now, maybe what you did or what you are going to do. Your mind is always talking to you in the form of thoughts that keep coming and going. It's like performing a soliloquy without letting anyone else know about it.

This voice in your head is the only sound that is devoid of emotions. You can't rebuke yourself and you cannot comfort yourself either. It is just some sluggish talk that takes the form of thoughts. You get away with it every time; even with the meanest words or the weirdest thoughts. You get away with these thoughts and words even when you say them out louder to yourself like when you are in a car and believe that others might think that you are singing or talking to someone over the phone.

You enjoy these simulations that recur all the time where you are neither the listener nor the one talking. You have several thoughts going on in your head when you are with people and even while you are talking. In fact, you talk more to some people when they are not with you. You have these continuous chatters that address the people in their absence by creating different scenarios. You are not the one talking, and you are not the one listening; it's like playing a dual-protagonist in a play and being the audience at the same time.

You can curse someone to their face while appearing pleasant to them, you secretly adore someone yet keep a cool face when they are around, and you imagine what you will do when the meeting is over while pretending to absorb everything that your boss says. You run these simulations every second of the day, like you are right now while reading this book. It's all natural, just don't get caught up and let the thoughts fly by focusing on this book.

Every day before you must do something important, you run a simulation in your head that shows how great you can do or how people will praise you. Sometimes, you run a thought and sometimes, you act it out but, in both cases, you are neither the actor nor the audience. You are not your thoughts nor your simulations, you are the very existence that sits here and feels these words right now. Your thoughts and simulations carry energy that can trigger a response based on how strongly you feel towards them.

It is likely that a person you hate might not be around you, yet his or her thought could make you so angry that your body temperature rises. At the same time, the thought of a loved one could bring out tears as a result of strong emotions. Try to remember something funny that might have happened to you and it will make you smile. Your thoughts have the power to make you laugh or cry because the energy associated with your thoughts have a strong impact on how you feel.

Your physical energy that you possess right now has everything to do with how your mind is working. You are calm and quietly reading this. Your feelings right now are directly linked to how aware you are at this moment or how your mind is working. Your mind that has the ability to make choices, you can stop reading right now or continue to find out what is coming.

The energy that you emit whether negative or positive is based on your level of consciousness. The waves emitted by your neurons are interrupted by the level of awareness that you bring in this moment. You can have a complete control over how you feel about an event or a thought by being more aware of it. On the other hand, you can also let a thought, or a person take control of your feelings and emit an uncontrolled emotion like anger.

Words, events, places, and people become energies in your mind. You can recall them anytime and when you do, they bring either positive or negative emotions. You control these emotions based on how much aware you are of you own presence.

I lifted my fingers and without opening my eyes, thought of my mother, I suddenly felt so much love that I could cry, I missed her so much. I then switched my thoughts to my father and felt nothing but sadness, I felt bad and scared but when I started observing why I was feeling this way, I could feel myself controlling my thoughts instead of letting them overpower me. I focused on my feelings and it felt strange that I have the choice to be aware of them. I could understand what the book was talking about. I pressed my fingers back on the words and started feeling the writing on the pages.

You can make a person your hero or villain based on how you feel towards him, just like you can make an experience a pleasant memory or a horrible recollection. This place where you are sitting has energy and your own presence has energy based on how you feel. You might be able to recall this moment sometime later and express how you felt reading me here.

Energy is equal to consciousness divided by feelings. Your energy goes into the negative zone when you let your feelings take control of you. On the contrary, the more consciously aware you are, the higher your spirits will be.

Your mind has an amazing energy that can hold the past and present together without disrupting your position. An event that triggered fear and contempt for you could have been a joyous memory for someone else. Your past is a recollection of energies rather than a set of memories. These recollections transform to a vacuum as consciousness emerges.

Since childhood, the concept of time and space has been hardwired into your brain, so you can relate your movement to the past and the present. The idea of space exists as a physical reality through your brain that can be felt around, and the idea of time exists in the form of energy that can be perceived by your thoughts. Your brain can relate to this physical space that you are sitting in right now so it's real, and the neurons that are in your brain are continuously emitting energy and storing energy right now.

Energy that doesn't have a physical visibility and the space that exists, both are then stored as clips in your brain as thoughts that are not supported with time. The energy in your neurons is strong enough to mobilize the electrons in your body and produce a response in the form of feelings. The energy, thoughts, and feelings are then captured in a time capsule, like photographs, and stay in your subconscious as a memory album.

Each memory has its own piece of space-time curvature with different feelings, whose magnitude can only be disrupted with consciousness. The stronger the level of consciousness, the weaker these emotional images will be.

The microtubules that are responsible for carrying energy within the cells, host the show for your energy system. But if you go down to the level of the microtubules, then there's an extremely good chance that you can get quantum-level activity inside them. At every moment, the activity in your brain is clustered with these multiple thoughts and images that can be triggered with any senses that bring a feeling that was felt when you experienced that image. For example, when you smell a pie, you remember the first time your mom baked one. All the memories associated with it come running back to you.

Your subconscious is always at work. Even while you are sleeping, you dream of what has or might have happened during the day or in the past. The subconscious energy is reduced only when it interacts with complete consciousness. You are then more aware of yourself and have more control over your feelings and thoughts. Your brain works through different energies, the energy that is within your brain and the actual reality that is the space around you. When you choose to focus on your reality and the energy of the cells that are involved in the present like your senses, only then you can be fully conscious and defeat the chatter that goes on in your mind.

When you choose to be the observer of your thoughts and your present moment, you refuse being the one who is observed and controlled; then you have the choice to either dwell in your subconscious, or live the reality by being more aware of your presence. It is all very strange and complicated when you have so many things happening in your subconscious, but it becomes very simple when you realize that the choice is your own and no one else's. It is like having two analogous states with different outcomes, so you choose to make life easy for you by reducing it to one. You can analyze your thoughts and life by interfering their energy with a higher energy of being aware of everything. If you learn to be more aware, then you do much better at life and making decisions.

Having continuous thoughts and an active subconscious is very natural, in fact, it would be unnatural if you didn't have them, but it gets disturbing only when you do not have a control over it. It disrupts your decision-making when your subconscious and memories bother you. Your energy overlaps when the lower energy of your sub-

consciousness interferes with the higher energy of the consciousness. The stream of consciousness and subconsciousness occur simultaneously, parallel to the physical reality.

Your subconscious with its lower energy is not insignificant. It bears significance about all the lessons you have learnt and all the memories that helped you solve the mysteries of life. But the feelings that are associated with them need not overpower you. Your subconscious acts like a co-pilot for the plane of your life, where the major decision-making lies with the real pilot of consciousness. You can be aware of your conscious beliefs, but you do not acknowledge the unconscious beliefs and thoughts that are at work most of the time. I will tell you a story now:

A man left his village with his daughter after his wife passed away. He wanted to go to his hometown, where everything didn't remind him of his wife. The father was very protective of his daughter and had always told her to stay away from men. She was not allowed to even talk to any boy in her childhood; the father was always scared for his reputation. While traveling, they came across a river on their way, where the girl saw a man who had just fallen into the river. He waved to be rescued, the girl looked back and saw her father slowly moving ahead. She thought by the time her father would reach there, the poor man would have drowned. So, she lent him a hand and pulled him out. The young man thanked the girl and departed. When her father came to see him thanking her for rescuing, he became mad with fury. The father even slapped her for letting her dress drench in water at the bottom. He yelled at her again after some time and cursed her for bringing a bad name to his reputation if someone found out. As they continued their way, the father was brooding and preoccupied. He was continuously lost in his thought and was having a bad time, while the daughter told him that it would be better for his health if they walked slowly. The father carried on with an angry face and cursed her again. When they reached the gate of his hometown, the girl looked in amazement for she had never been out of her village.

"It is so beautiful, and I am glad we came here for a change," the girl told her father.

"I cannot believe that you didn't wait for me or ask for help. This is how you react after seeing a man, even though you know you are not supposed to touch any man. It is insolent. You are disrespectful," he told her in anger.

"Father," the girl replied, "I let go of his hand a long time back while you are still holding it with you."

The man wondered at what his daughter had told him for a long while...

You see, how holding on to negative emotions can impact your behavior. You live your lives through a reactive state of being, meaning when things happen to you, they determine how you feel and, as a result, control you. Your thoughts, your beliefs, and your recurring thoughts are what makes up your life. The subconscious mind is operating about ninety-percent of the time to help you make decisions, but the problem is that you do better when you use your conscious mind as a decision-making tool.

The conscious is at a higher energy frequency that brings more energy to your life, but it could be sabotaged by the doubts of the subconscious. So, you are not able to control your life or make sane decisions. You always hear that change your thoughts to change your destiny because it is only through a control of the subconscious mind and the thoughts in your head that you can utilize the power of your conscious mind. In order to be more conscious of the things around you or happening in your life, you need to understand the voices of your subconscious first. Fight any doubts and deal with any concerns that these thoughts bear.

Consciousness without the subconscious is not enough. Though consciousness bears a much higher energy that gives better results, we need the subconscious to fully function in life. If you woke up one day consciously without any subconscious mind, you would not be able to identify who you are. You need the memories, the feelings, and all the energy, whether low or high, to live a life of awareness.

Your subconscious is a storage bank that never shuts off; subconscious is a land with feelings, with the memories that you cherish, and recollections that you fear. 'Feeling' is the word we use to describe our conscious vibration. Emotion is your energy in motion. Everything about you and around you are in motion. You are here with your brain constantly trying to read and understand my words. Your heart and inner system are doing their best right now to keep you alive and breathing. Your brain tells you to keep holding this book as you read with so many molecules at work inside and outside of you, everything that is in motion generates vibration.

You are a mass of liveliness that functions on frequencies and vibrations. And whether you realize it or not, you are giving out energy all the time. Your subconscious mind, your feelings, and your conscious existence are all working together simultaneously, and nothing is at rest. You always act according to the vibration that your energy gives. The world around you comprises of three things; the subconscious, the conscious, and your own body. Your body is the tool of energy that feels, senses, and acts. There is an infinite number of frequencies and the higher frequencies of the conscious world are connected to the lower vibrations of the subconscious. Your thoughts and your feelings interfere with these frequencies with their own vibrations. The more control you have over your feelings, thoughts, and subconscious, the better you can tune into the higher frequency of consciousness.

It is what you impress upon the subconscious that controls the frequency of your energy. The frequency is the energy that you are emitting and operating your life on. If you are operating on a negative energy, you feel sad and low. Feeling is the word that we have intended to describe our conscious awareness of the vibration we are in, but your conscious awareness can be altered with a will to change your energy. That willingness is what makes up your ability to be aware. It can be done with a snap of the fingers; all you need is the will to do it. For the rest of the time your subconscious is at play, it is continuously active, even without your will. It is like the universal mind that controls your life in the background. It cannot differentiate between what is imagined or real. Just remember that if your feelings are at play, and your emotions are involved in what lies here, then it is real for the mind.

You must learn to enter the subconscious and explore the truth behind your feelings in order to fully control them. I will take you on a venture to explore your subconscious, so that understanding why you feel and do certain things becomes easier for you.

I was captivated, fascinated, almost in a spell; elated to another reality. I lifted my fingers from the fine metallic words that had started to feel warm with my touch. My hand held this amazing book and I glanced over these amazing words that could change my life forever. The book had a powerful grip on my mind, its genial reality began to distort the fake ideas my mind held; challenging the once ordinary realities of my existence, bringing me into a new raging land, where even my sense of self was highly questionable.

I thought I needed to take a break or two to fully absorb in the new information. I could feel my breath and sense the air around me. I was trying to separate my thoughts from my reality. I needed to calm my mind more because I could see that my mind drifted back to thinking if I didn't observe it.

What was this subconscious? I thought to myself. It was amazing that I could watch my own self and assess why I had these thoughts. I slowly closed the book, sliding across the warm velvet, I held it for a while just gazing on this red color, it resembled a scarf that was given to me by my mom. I remember it was a wonderful gift, I got it on my graduation. *Oh my God, I am thinking about the past and this book cover acted like a trigger to bring back a memory that I had.* Wow, observing my thoughts and why I had them, was amazing. I placed the book on the side table by the lamp. I felt my lips opening to yawn, I stretched my arms above my head and lay down to rest. I was trying to analyze every thought that came to my mind as I drifted to a sound slumber, slowly and then all at once.

Chapter 5

I forgot to turn off my alarm and when it went off, I woke up suddenly with a fast-beating heart and a buzzing in my head. I needed a moment to shed the anxiety from my shivering body. I turned off the alarm and could go back to sleep, yet I took a moment to bring myself back to reality. I burrowed into the warm, soft sheets for a while and gazed out of the window at the changing sky. The sky seemed to be covered with clouds, reminding me of my mornings in New York. By the time my eyes were awake, my brain was overwhelmed with the thoughts from last night's reading. Any thought that my subconscious brought to me was questioned by my brain and I was brought back to my present.

I got out of my bed and freshened up quickly, I couldn't wait to get back to the book. I was free the whole day so instead of going out, I made myself a warm breakfast in my tiny kitchen-like corner, and sat down to wonder about the book again. I sat across the room and stared at the book lying on the night stand. It sat heavily wrapped up in its warm cover, with the words beaming off its surface. There was something striking about it that was inviting me to seek the answers that needed to be explored.

As soon as I finished eating, I took the book and crept back into my cliquey sheets. The book had enchanted my senses, when I was holding it, I realized that it felt heavier than it looked. I always had to pick it up with both hands. I got comfy in my bed and continued from where I had left last night.

Your subconscious that preserves your imagination through feelings is very powerful. The words that I write are not only seen, but also felt by your mind. If I say a red flower, you not only read it, but your mind shows you one too. Your subconscious cannot differentiate between what you have imagined and what has happened, it just preserves those pictures as memories. Your feelings associated with these memories give them the energy that vibrates through you. You have this past in your mind, and you have these dreams about your future that only you can see. The energy that they give is visible to you only. Your senses cannot see what your feelings hold. The feelings associated with your past, present, and future reside in your subconscious. Wherever you are in your life, is a result of all these feelings, thoughts, and actions, and where you are not, is also because of the actions you took as a result of these feelings.

So, where do you want to be in your life, come and explore your feelings, so they don't interfere with the higher frequency of your conscious self, and make the decisions that will vibrate with the dream of your future. The vibrations of the negative feelings can never resonate with the positivity of the imagined future.

Turn this page and move into the land of the subconscious and encounter the feelings that you don't see.

I lifted my fingers and turned the page; I was about to place my fingers on the letters when I felt like the room was getting colder. Maybe I should turn on the heating.

As I open my eyes, I am seeing darkness all around, I am not hearing the clock's ticking. I am standing on my feet and my shoes are not able to hold the coldness that creeps through the cold floor. My legs are feeling weaker and my stomach is rumbling for I know that I am not in my room anymore. The silence is strong enough to make my breathing seem noisy and my heart is pounding fists against my chest. I am pinching myself again to wake myself up but it sure is not a dream. I am gathering the courage to walk forward. My eyes are getting wider than ever, trying to figure out a way or look for a dying light. My body is telling me to run faster than ever, but I am walking slowly, with my arms stretching through the dark. I am feeling a sudden gush of respite, when my eyes catch an opening slit with a yellow light beaming through.

I move towards the light and feel the curtains that enclose this light. I try to peep through the slit enclosed by these huge curtains, my adrenalin surges so fast that I feel like I could throw up. I hold the sides of both these curtains and peek through the slit.

The bright light comes from the huge chandelier that hangs high above, where there seems to be no roof. The room seems like an inside of a huge castle with no walls or roof, but the light from the gigantic chandelier extending to wherever my eyes could see. I look all the way up but it's hard to look directly at the light that is bright like the sun. I squint a little and part the curtains a bit more to look around.

"It didn't take you long to reach here," says a tall figure dressed in off-white, as he walks towards me.

I am about to close the curtains and run to, I don't know where, as he gets hold of my arm and helps me move forward.

"I am going to take you to our white circle, and you can help yourself with something," he tells me, as we glide through the long hallway.

Some figures in faded yellow pass by me, "Oh, she is here. We were told that she might visit us."

I hear chatters and look around in bewilderment, hoping it all to end up like a dream. I pinch myself again but I feel like I am being held hostage and dragged against my will.

The man helps me to a seat which he places by a man sitting on a very high chair. "You will sit here, beside Lord Wise."

"I am glad you came to visit," Lord Wise nods at me. He is a tall and handsome man in a clean white robe, sitting on a high chair that is parallel to another chair, where a lady sits in a bright white dress and smiles at me. Three people in off-white robes are sitting on less high chairs in front of us.

I quietly settle into my chair and look around. It is hard to define everyone around me as people, for they look like tall humans with perfect figures, dressed in long robes. I am facing what looks like to be some conference of people without tables. There are people in pink on the right and in grey on the left, while a bunch of yellows sit across us and the middle is an open space where these faded robes seem to be gliding across and serving their respective circles food and drinks.

"Here, have something to swallow down your throat and relax." The same man in faded white comes to me with a tray, holding an orange juice. I take it with shivering hands that are sore cold now, and he then softly glides to stand by my side. There is another woman robed in faded white, serving the lady in bright white, while the red and black circles have many women and men serving in pink and grey. Though the seats are arranged more like rectangles than circles, the people serving them address them as circles.

"Yes, the bitter berries were for the black circle," smiles a lady in pink to herself as she walks by me. I take a sip from my juice and it's like my mouth and gut are being refreshed with life. It is so fresh and delicious. I drink some

more to feel better. I take some more juice to calm myself as I feel alone and forlorn, though I am surrounded with all sorts of people. It is strange that the white circle is quiet and more observant than the rest.

I gain some sense to start looking around me and observing everyone. The feeling of strangeness is overbearing, yet all the people look at me and then ignore me like they already knew me. The bright light feels like a fiery mist above an endless meadow, it is getting warmer and I can feel my hands again. I am slowly waking up from the dream-like enchantment and hearing the fading whispers more clearly.

"You have to stay hopeful, as long as you don't find the answer," the lady in the pink circle smiled at the other lady sitting with her.

"It is a pity I still have to put up with all the drama, even though I am better than everyone else." A voice came from the yellow circle.

"What an unpleasant taste, I feel the sweetness of the berry is sticking to my throat." A man from the grey circle frowned at his server.

I wonder at all these people, trying to be as calm as I can be. I notice that the people around me are not actually walking, but floating very close to the earth.

Lord Wise rises above his seat and everything is quiet, there is no sound and everyone freezes where they are. He is a huge man who seems a lot taller than I had expected, the fire was on his face like summer-light upon the ocean.

His hair is so white that they seem to match his bright robe. His robes are flowing about him and it looks like he is wearing a cloak. He wears a bright golden flower around his neck that looks like a big golden button from far. He stands still, enchanting, while everyone looks at him without saying or moving.

"Here, my friend, is yet another human, Meryl, the child of Afua and Jules R. Eden." Lord Wise points towards me and I feel that my heartbeat is faster than ever now. He knows my name too and my parents and if I am a human, then what are they? I am getting scared as I imagine them to be something other than just humans. The lady in white rises and says something slowly to Wise.

"You are right, Lady Wise," he looks at me and the light of his eyes fall on me, piercing through my heart. "This here, is the red circle, where you see different feelings clad in pink robes. They are some of the descendants of Love," he points with his right hand to the right side, all the people here have different skin tones and other than their robes, the only feature that they share is the dull shade of red hair. They smile at me as I swallow my nervousness in my throat.

"Here, on our left, is the black circle where you will see some of the descendants of Fear," he points to them with his left hand and I can see them nodding at me, though they do not frown, but I feel a sudden gush of hot blood flushing through my brain. Their most prominent feature is their dark hair that contrasts with different skin tones. He then points out that the people seated across were few of

the descendants of Ego who have agreed to be a part of this meeting. I try to swallow my emotions again, but something seems to be stuck in my throat.

"You did the right thing by choosing to come here," says Wise to me, and then turns to others, "Descendants of all the mighty feelings, I say this with great pleasure, that the number of humans visiting our land is increasing, and they all seek nothing but the truth. We are the survivors from a time that tested our abilities till we had almost perished. We too once, were lost, like they are now. We see humans struggling from time to time to survive in their world, just like we once did. From time to time, we have seen the greatest world leaders or great saints, and humans visit us, but now the ordinary human seeks his authenticity too. Since we are very close to the humans and we have always helped them understand their reality, the task of helping these wonderers once again falls on us. Only this time, we are seeing an increase in their number. The people visiting the land of sub-conscious is increasing day by day, so we need more strength from all of you; more than ever. And now, once again, the task of helping these humans falls upon us. We may not be visible to the ordinary human eye, yet we have always seen their struggle and proved our loyalty whenever they have needed us." Lord Wise pauses and sees that I am sitting in utter bewilderment.

"You are not alone. Your search to find the truth of your life is a part of the struggle of every human we see. You will learn all that you need to defeat your weaknesses and earn your strengths. Things that have been hidden from you shall be dawned with wisdom, so that you may

understand your reality. Your job is to make a wise choice every time you are tested." I tremble again, when I see him focused at me. There is pin-drop silence, and everyone is focused on what Wise has to say.

"There was a time when we were betrayed and learned to survive just in time to save our race from perishing. The humans too, have been infected with the same betrayal and strive to bring balance to their reality. History has been repeated many times and heroes have been reborn with their passion for surviving and bringing more reality to their world. With the increase in number of humans striving to bring peace to their world, their foe gains strength too. At the same time, our job to help them is getting tough. We, as always, shall unite to work harder and help these lost humans survive their own realities, so their race does not face termination like we once did. You all stand with me?"

Lady Wise rises from her seat, nods at Mr. Wise, and stands by his side.

A man from the right side rises to speak to us, "I, Amour, the fourth descendant of love, welcome you to our land of beauty and love where we will help you find the sweet sense of living with peace and delight. We shall work hard to help you find the true passion of your life that you so eagerly desire." His skin is slightly darker than the people of his circle, with the same shade of dark, red hair. They all nod towards me and I feel like I can smile or maybe, I feel that I should smile, so I do. They have this sense of calmness about them. They all smile back, and I feel like I can breathe without holding half of my breath in.

I let out a strong exhale and become comfortable in my seat.

"In this hour of need, I, Peur, the fifth descendant of fear, assure you that we shall help you see all the ugliness that bounds you to your doubts and worries." *A woman rises from the left side to show herself.* "There isn't much to love in this world, you will see why we exist. You may have to give in to your fear." *Her very fair complexion presents a contrast to her very dark hair and eyebrows. She speaks with raised eyebrows and all the people in her circle look at me with disappointment and distress. I suddenly feel low and nod a little as my eyes get bigger.*

"Surely, your fear should not overestimate itself when your ego is there to find excuses for yourself. I am Fierte, the third descendant of ego, and I will make sure that you see how your selfishness proves to be the only worthy attribute." *The man has a tanned complexion with the distinct feature of yellow hair. His smirk is the common element feature that he shares with his circle.*

"So, you alone are enough to help her explore the reality, from your circle," *said Peur with a frown.*

"Of course, you can challenge me alone against the whole of your circle, I will prove my word," *Fierte coldly sneers…*

"Enough," *Lord Wise snaps at them, there is a change in his voice, and it is powerful enough to make others tremble. It seems like the light from the chandelier seemed to be dimmer for a second when his words flashed across the hall. He rises a bit higher and looks at the yellow circle.*

All the feelings settle calmly in their seats. Wise slowly relaxes his body and comes down. The change in his voice is astounding.

"Do not let the shadow that once blinded you, creep beneath your motives, to help the mankind and overrule your judgements. I foresee a light of wisdom prevailing for the humans and their race shall not perish, as long as they seek our help. Let not your dark nature steep into your objectives to free these people from their miseries. You all shall stand in unity and serve your roles when you are asked to." His voice is getting softer and he comes to me. However, he is very close to me, it feels like he is taking some time to come closer. Though I have always considered myself a very tall woman, he is a lot taller than me. I stand up, shaking in my body. He bends on his knees to come to my equal and speaks softly.

"You shall face many challenges along your way here. No one is your true friend, and no one is your true enemy, you have to decide and learn to make your own choices, in order to pass everything." He holds my hand and I can barely feel his touch; it is as though my hand is hanging in the air. "I am Wisdom, your friend and the fighter of your foes, I shall be there for you the whole way along. It is up to you to seek my help." My eyes fall on his golden amulet and its shine flashes on my eyes. I squeeze my eyes and can't open them.

I relaxed my eyes and then made an effort to open them, just to see myself sitting in my room, with my fingertips touching the golden circle shaped like a flower in the book. I took a sigh of relief after looking around. The imagery of the book had been very heavy for me. I felt a burden had been lifted and I was able to breathe easily.

Chapter 6

The multiple talking in my head now seemed to be passive to the reality advocating my consciousness. I thought it would be a small building, but everything was the opposite of what I had expected, the church was beautiful. Its ceiling with the most dramatically beautiful design seemed to be stretching across. I gazed in wonder at the wonderful exhibition of art, rotating my head in every direction.

"Thank you for meeting with us," said Emre, while we stood up to greet the pastor.

He was a very old man in a long white robe with a rosary in his hands. He stood near the altar and looked at all of us with a deep concern, observing us from head to toe. He was assisted by another man who was a little shorter than him and had a slightly pale complexion.

"We are glad to have you here. How can I offer to be of service to the foreigners who have come to the house of our worship, bearing the message of peace?" the pastor replied in a loud voice, still examining our appearances. He had a fair skin with a few freckles and a very strong French accent, while he spoke in English.

We slowly approached the place where the pastor stood with his assistant, "I know that running the church is a full-time job and it is kind of you to –"

"Get to the point, Mister," his assistant said quickly, looking at us like he was running short of time. "We didn't interrupt our day just so you could tell us about how important our job is." He looked shorter than he was, and his jet-black hair complemented his pastel skin. His English was better with a strong accent.

"Very well then, I have come here to be a part of the peace mission and message that every religious sector aims to spread through the people that go there. I am Emre, and this is my team, Meryland Chris." He pointed towards us and we nodded as Emre introduced us.

"Mr. Emre, I appreciate that," said the pastor calmly, "Every religious institute needs the people who support peace and it's not easy to do what we do, but we have a whole team to perform these duties. This here is my assistant, Joshua Berko, he is also the minister of youth here, and specializes the ministry of youth's work."

"We are professors from different universities, and we travel around the world to not only deliver the message of peace, but make a difference in people's lives. We are here for only a few months as part of our UNV program, but I assure you that by the time we decide to leave, you will want us to stay more." Emre was trying to negotiate on friendly terms.

"How did you come to know about our mission, or should I say, why did you choose us for this reason? You could have gone anywhere in Paris or the world and offered your skills." Joshua had a very strict tone.

"Because we didn't spend our time trying to interrupt your day, we do our homework and we know that the mission of the people who work here is just more than worship." Chris came forward and asserted with a casual attitude, "You like to spread the message of peace and in fact, some of the people that you train for your youth program want to join the government's peace programs."

"It would be easy to trust you, Mr. Chris, but how do we know that you guys are not some sorts of agents or working with some other department who have come to gather some dirt. After all, you did come here a few days back with a friend of yours who claimed to be a photographer," Joshua asserted, staring at Chris. "We like to do our homework too."

"My team works on its projects seriously and we needed those pictures for a few articles. Our photographer is a local photographer here at a French magazine. We are professors from individual countries and we just want to be a part of the peace campaign that our universities run." Emre had an air of calmness about him no matter what. "Look, our security checks have already been cleared before coming here and what we want from you is just a chance to be a part of your mission for a few months. You have everything that you need to know about us."

"We already have a team here and we are very good at what we do." Joshua was still looking at Chris while the pastor just observed everyone, twisting the rosary in his hands.

"No doubt to that, but somehow in the past, the people over here have been under questioning after the terrorist attacks and civil disobedience movements," Chris explained his point.

Emre continued with a straight face, "Maybe you want someone who has seen you do your job and still wants to work with you and if it ever comes to any questioning, we can always clarify your position, for we are volunteers with the sole mission to spread peace."

The pastor raised his hand to end the argument.

"No one here has any involvement in anything other than what is right for the humanity. Every good soul is welcome to share that," the pastor asserted with a firm hand.

"Then give us a chance to be a part of that right and welcome our request to share that too."

"Do you think your message is strong enough to do what we couldn't?"

"I believe that you can give a chance to someone who embodies in person what you preach in spirit, for if there is even a one percent chance of making a positive influence, we believe in taking it, rather than doing nothing."

"You are pretty sure of yourself."

"I see an opportunity here, where the doors have always been open for people in need."

"You know us well and for what it's worth, I will let you have a day or two in the week, pick a day, and be a part of what we preach. We run many programs for spreading the message of peace, you can take part to improve the youth education program with your lectures, but if I see no result, feel free to go back." The pastor nodded and left us to meet someone else who was waiting for him with a parcel. Joshua shook Emre's hand with an unease and left us.

Everyone had faults and flukes, I thought to myself, and if they were all refined out, then trust wouldn't be a choice. Like with Emre, who was too perfect to be untrusted. I wondered, but my mind wouldn't let me. I was jerked into facing the present, even though my mind drifted into some weird thoughts, my senses brought me back to where I was standing. I realized that I was becoming more aware of my presence without even trying.

Chapter 7

I guess it's human nature to love or want something you have never had, even if it was the only thing that was missing in your life. Instead of focusing on all that we have, we yearn for the one thing we cannot or do not have. If it's not the case with everyone, it certainly was true for me.

After walking the stage, turning from a graduand to a graduate and hearing people congratulate me, I still wished if my father could be there too, with my mother. Maybe because most of my friends had both their parents cheering for them and Samantha, who followed me in the row, was waving at her parents too. Though her dad cheering for me was something he had always done at every occasion, but today, it made me feel like he was overcompensating.

My mom was taking many pictures of me and Samantha's dad cheered for both of us but deep inside, I wish he wouldn't do that. Just not today, I had no idea why I felt this way, but I wish he would just cheer his own daughter. Everyone knew he was her dad and his cheering for me made it obvious that my own dad was nowhere around.

My mother was staring at her camera proudly as I walked down the stage. She waved to me with tears in her eyes and shaking her camera with a rich smile. She would be living this moment again and again through the pictures that she had captured. She had seized the moment forever to live by. A memory she would hold forever on her walls for the people, and in her heart for her own sake.

Even after the ceremony, my mom took pictures of me with all my friends and Samantha's family. The day of truth was finally here, the stepping stone revealing what we had been preparing for.

"Hey, Mary, you left your cap at your seat," said Joseph, the boy who hung out with girls mostly to avoid boys. "Who leaves this? You can be happy for yourself too, you know." He smirked.

"Thanks, Joseph," I took my cap from him and saw him staring at me to say something, "Would you like to join us for the picture?" I asked him half-heartedly.

"Is that your real mom?" Joseph asked me slowly.

"Yes, why is it surprising that my mom is a black lady?" I said, raising my eyebrows.

"No, I mean, I kind of thought you were Mexican or something."

I was used to this kind of questioning because I had different features from the other half-black people. I wouldn't understand it when I was little but now it was usual for me.

"Mom, enough with the pictures, let's go home now." I gestured my mom to stop.

"I want to capture everything about this day," my mom could not help her broad smile, "But fine, fine, I will stop for a while, it's your day and I am so happy for you." My mom came close to hug me again. "If it were for me, I would be shouting out to the world, but I see that you would be asking me to stop again."

"No doubt to that," said Katrina, "Meryl always has a stick up her ass, but why are you so stiff today, man? I feel free as a bird, no more being a kid, we are officially adults now."

"You are still too immature to be considered adult, Katy." Samantha forced her way between me and Katrina. "One more picture, please."

And my mom quickly stood in front of us to capture the moment.

"Your mom was looking for you, Kat," Samantha said slowly to Katrina.

"Oh no, why didn't you tell me before?" Katrina ran back to meet her mom.

"I will see you guys at the park in the evening, take care." Joseph left to join some other group.

"I will surely miss these awkward friendships here," Samantha whispered, but I had no idea what she meant.

"What an amazing day to be remembered by all of us." Samantha's father came to join us, followed by her mother. Samantha's mother took a moment to smile at us and then got busy with her mobile again. She was mostly busy over the phone, talking about her business. She didn't talk much with anyone who was around her because she was mostly committed to her mobile. My mom took our pictures with Samantha's father, but her mom went on the side to take a call. If I were not friends with Samantha, it would be very easy to hate her mom, who had hardly ever spent any time with us on any occasion.

"I am so proud of both of you," said her father.

"Yes, Mr. Remy, but you must be prouder of your own daughter for sure," I said, swiftly pointing out that my father was not there.

"Meryl and Samantha, you both make me happy and proud," my mom said quickly, to cover up the gloomy attitude I was holding. "We have a surprise for both of you."

"I thought we were going to wait till the end of the day," said Mr. Remy, "Are you sure we should just hand it out to them?"

"What is it?" said Samantha, getting more excited than she had been for the ceremony, "Come on, you guys will not make us wait for it anymore."

"Now that you have revealed it, I guess I will have to give it to them." He held out two envelopes and gave them to us.

They were confirmation letters from the McGill University. I was delighted at last, we had both wanted to be lawyers and this was the first step towards achieving our dreams. Samantha screamed with joy and we all had a group hug for this was the moment worth waiting for.

"I am so happy that both of you would be going to the same university and I am happier that you have chosen to stay close to me." My mom started crying again.

One beep and then another, I wake up to the sound of yet another text messages. In the heaviness of my slumber, I slowly open my eyes. I do not rush to look around for now I know that everything about my mom is a dream. I wanted to make the memory last longer, I did not want her love to fade away like a memory and I could still feel my hand in hers. Her cheering voice lighting up my dull moments and her love reforming my presence. After being away for years, I now knew that it was a dream, even while I had it. My mom had become a memory and her love, a yearning that I chose to turn away.

I had slept on my sofa again, I checked my messages to see that Emre had finalized our meeting to be scheduled on every Tuesday now, and the head office had confirmed receiving my report of today's meeting. I went to my bed but did not feel like sleeping, my thoughts wanted to keep me awake but I was noticing them, which reminded me of the effect the book was having on me.

I slid into my bed and grabbed the huge red book with both hands. I opened it and turned to where I had left it the last time.

Chapter 8

I stare into the darkness that surrounds me, widening my eyes as much as I can, when I spot a yellow flicker on my right side. Bobbing up and down unevenly, a stick appears below it. It is a long and thin candle; its light is faint, yet bright enough to reflect onto the face of the person holding it. I cannot figure out who this is, yet I hold on tight to my chair. I am sitting on what feels like a rocking chair with strong wooden arms. He seems to be going forward with the candle and holds it close to another one.

The two flames illuminate the soft features of its bearer and he lights three more candles on the stand slightly above his head. He has a smile on his face and when the candle lights are bright enough to light up my surroundings, I feel like I am sitting in my own room that is just empty, now with only two chairs and this shelf bearing the candles. The man turns towards me and sits on the chair opposite to me. He has a smile on his face and a sense of calmness about him. I realize that he is the man I saw the last time, who introduced himself as the descendant of love.

"I hope you are feeling better than the last time you tried to reach your subconscious land," says Amour, as he settles into his chair, "The first time is always hard to absorb, but you will get better after the second tour. In fact, you will be a consella sooner than you know."

"What is a consella?" I ask him with a surprise.

"Consellas are consciously aware humans who can sense their own feelings and of those around them. They stand out in a crowd and perceive things better than the ugnasters."

"Ugnasters?" I raise my eyebrows.

"Yes, the people who are mostly drowned by their own thoughts, unaware of the reality around them, they exuberate a very low energy." Amour smiles as he twitches his nose, "I don't blame them, it's human nature to be tempted by your own thoughts and feelings to overlook what is in front of you and imagine what is not."

I nod my head as I look around in wonder, "This place looks a lot like my own room, where I was sitting while reading the book."

"Yes, you didn't have to go far, as you were practicing, being aware since your last visit to the subconscious and you have generated some positive energy around you, so the feelings of love are easily accessible," Amour tells me to comfort me.

"Are you saying that you exist all the time and we can't see you?"

"We exist based on your level of energy, if you have high energy, then feelings of love stay close by you and if you choose to side with fear, then its descendants surround you."

"Then why can't we see you?"

"The reason is that just as the human ears cannot detect acoustic signals outside of a certain range, similarly the human vision sensors are tuned to a certain wavelength," Amour explains to me.

"So, we cannot hear or see you?"

"Not anymore. Not since the feelings lost their strength to keep the balance that supported their existence."

"You mean, we could before?"

"Let's just say a long time ago, when the feelings were strong enough and the humans were naïve enough, we could have co-existed in harmony."

"Why did you lose your touch?" *I am getting curious now.*

"That is the reason you are here today. I will tell you the story of the prehistoric times, when the feelings existed with strength and power. Your job is to focus on understanding it, to utilize it, and help yourself become more aware of it." Amour leans towards me, "I want you to understand how you can become more aware of your emotions, while we enjoy our tea."

"Tea?" I ask him in a surprise, and he points to the cup of tea that rests on the side table beside me. This table is like the one I have in my room for working with the laptop. I look back at him and he is holding a cup himself. "Is this some kind of magic?"

"Not exactly, it's the land of the subconscious where you create through your imagination." Amour raises his cup of tea to me and I take hold of my tea cup.

We all come from the energy that runs through our lives from day to day, descending since the beginning of times, coursing its way into the future like the genes that are inherited. This energy flows through, like a river with highs and lows, waving love and fear along its banks. One moment of fear or love pounding on to make a ripple effect for those that surround it, the river of energy is unstoppable till it rises to drown all those that come in its way.

Once again, its energy is on the rise, marking the ascend of a new era, and the shaping of history. With the rise of its flow, the species bearing the higher energy will survive those bearing the lower energy. Just like the species of feelings that once ruled a world were saved by their choices to preserve their energy, there will be a test for everyone to be aware of their choices. Those were the species, embodying prominent feelings with consenzi, high energy, and ugowen, low energy; marking clear distinction between love and hate, joy and fear, trust and betrayal, and so on. There was no confusion as to what is right and wrong.

It is believed that before the hell conspired against the heavens and before there was a life to be found anywhere, the consenzi of the sun helped nourish a seedling that bore the most amazing flower from the greener of the grasses. The flower was as red as the color of the human blood. The sun colluded with the winds and water to create a bubble around that red flower for seven days.

On the seventh day, a glimpse of rainbow popped the bubble to reveal the most beautiful creature with all that was good in nature. It was so beautiful that the sun, water, and everything in nature were astonished at the outcome of putting out their best consenzi. It was a beautiful creature with an air of charisma around her. Her beauty could not conceal all the emotions that she carried within. Everything in nature agreed to call her Love, for that seemed to be what she was exuberating. The womanly creature was not a being, but a feeling, a figure of love, and everything good. Love travelled on that planet with the utmost grace and it was no wonder that anything that came in her presence seemed to be blessed with her consenzi.

Love wanted more to adore, so she asked nature to provide her someone that would serve her, and she could nourish under her love and charm, for she felt lonely doing everything by herself. The sun told her that they had used up their highest consenzi to create Love, but Love still felt lonely, so the wind whispered in her ears to plant a seed after one year and let it grow for seven days on the darker soil, where there was no light, just damp, dark mud for if Love wanted someone to serve her, she would have to make that grow out of the ugowen.

Love waited a whole year living off the land and blessing it with her consenzi, till she planted the seed in the dark, where no light and wind could reach it and after seven days, the mud bubble popped to release a creature that had the most mysterious presence, who could spike fear in anyone that turned to it. He gazed at Love with astonishment, for it was difficult to not stare at her beauty, but Love was taken back as she had not expected a being with so much negative ugowen about him. He was not ugly, yet his appearance had a strong fearsome quality to it. Love felt afraid yet, she went towards him, with a smile and charisma that was in her nature. She floated along in her red robes.

"I was instructed to plant a seed if I wanted someone to help me around, but I had no idea it would be someone so different than me," said Love with a tint of joy and love, for that was all that she could feel.

"I am at your service," said the individual, bowing down.

Love knew that he had a very different energy than hers. His dark hair and fair complexion presented a contrast to his black robe. She knew that he possessed very low ugowen and looked fearful, but she was incapable of feeling anything other than love. She gave him the name Fear, and they both floated across the land, with Fear following Love in obedience.

Love cherished the sun, nature, and the lovely sights where Fear would serve her wishes with a bowed head, yet he would sneak into dark corners whenever he found time. Love saw that she did not have a companion, for they were as different as night and day, and had nothing in common.

After a year, Love asked the nature to make another feeling like her, but the sun told her that it was not possible. There could never be something like Love; she had the greatest consenzi. Seeing her sad, the wind pitied her once again and took her to the mountain where her seed was planted on the green top. Here, the wind took the form of a cloud and spoke to Love once again.

"Plant a seed here and I will nourish it with all the help that I can get," the wind-cloud spoke, while changing shapes.

"I want someone like me who has the same interests in life," said Love with a smile.

"It is not possible to create another you, but what we can do, is to help you create a feeling that is the like of you, I will help to create someone with a good consenzi." The wind-cloud then faded into a smoke and flew away.

After seven days, a light bubble popped and a creature in faded pink walked out, bearing a consenzi. Love could feel the energy around him and was glad to have found a feeling of likeness. She called him Joy, and floated across the land with him, enjoying her love for light and nature. Fear served them when he was needed but after sometime, asked Love to help him find someone for his company too. Love asked him to plant a seed like the wind had told her to, but he would have to do it at a dark place, like the mud that bore his own flower. Love would ask the wind to help Fear too.

When Fear found the flower after seven days, a creature of fearful sight came out of the black bubble. She was dreadful and fearful, with a negative ugowen just like him. The blackness of her hair and eyebrows radiated against her fair skin. She was beautiful, yet dreadful, seeming fearful. Fear was glad to have found someone he could fly around in the dark lands with. She was called Anger by everyone. They would appear to serve Love and Joy when they were needed and obliged their roles, for they knew that they were inferior to Love and were made to serve Love and her partners.

Years passed by, and Love was favored with a partner feeling, with the help of wind and her colluders. Similarly, Fear was awarded with a partner for all the work that he and his fellows did for the consenzis. Thus, it was established that every year, a man and woman of consenzi and ugowen would plant a seedling in their respective spots, and nourish the feeling that they helped bring to life. Love would bless all the feelings despite their energy. Life went on like this, living in peace, with a clear distinction of the high and low, where no one interfered. Without the richness of feelings and emotions, there wouldn't be a world to exist, so there they lived, increasing in numbers, and supporting each other. They managed to create little homelands for themselves on the mountain-tops filled with consenzi, where the feelings dressed in black would come to serve from the valley of Ugowen. And every year, one seed would be planted on the top and another in the valley by the feelings that took to each other's liking. Love would bless them after seven days and they would all celebrate the birth of a new addition.

"Then why did those feelings extinct?" I ask Amour, sipping the most delicious blend of flavors from my cup.

"We did not become extinct; we just came to live here after we were too weak to survive on our planet. We came at a place where the normal eye cannot see us till you learn to activate your subconscious through the conscious world." Amour's words confused me.

"And, we can all see you in our minds?"

"No, only those who master their consciousness are able to control their subconscious land and see us there."

"So, I have mastered my subconscious?"

"Not yet, but you are helped by someone who has, and this book is a present from him. You will have to face a few challenges before you can control your subconscious or master your consciousness. Till then, everything is a test for you."

"I want to know that if everything was fine and Love dominated the land of feelings where no one from Fear's side crossed the boundaries, then why did feelings lose their charisma and fade into our subconscious land with low energy?" I ask and lean back, waiting to hear more.

It is said that Pride was the most beautiful feeling, dwelling in the Ugowen. Pride, though less graceful, had an aura of magnificence, like Love. She was beautiful with a little dark skin and jet-black hair. She was the fruit of the seed planted by Greed and Lust. They had raised her with all the lust and greediness. Doubt and Envy took to her liking, and wanted to plant the seed of ugowen with her, but Pride was too stubborn to be persuaded, she thought she needed a feeling better than those dwelling in the Ugowen, for she was too important to be there in the first place. She belonged at a place where she too, was served by ugowens.

A huge tree now stood on the mountain top where Love planted the positive feelings. Love would go to pray to the nature here and ask them to help her in blessing her fellows. She would go to ask for nature's help before starting the festival of growth every year. While she was standing there with her long red robe flowing about her and her eyelids closed, wind started blowing strongly around her.

"I see a collusion of the Ugowen and Consenzi happening soon," the wind whispered to Love.

Love opened her eyes to find a cloud of wind in front of her on top of the tree.

"That is not possible, the feelings do not like their opposites, and it has never happened before, for that is how the balance between the light and dark is maintained," Love assured the wind.

"It has been prophesied, my dear, that a feeling of the dark shall collude with the one from your side of the land and the product of that seed shall be the start of the doom for your people." Wind was changing shapes all the while it talked to love.

"That cannot be, you have to help me, help me stop it," Love asked Wind.

"I cannot help you in what is to come for you that has been prophesied by the universe, it is meant to happen, just like you were meant to be created."

"Then, at least help me identify that feeling so I can keep it under check and look out for my people," Love begged nature for help.

"There is one thing that I can help you with. As you know that all the feelings bearing love smile after looking at their reflection because it's beautiful and all the feelings bearing fear abhor their ugly reflections, so they utter a cry of despair when they see theirs. It has been told that the feeling that will be responsible for the doom shall have an ugly reflection," wind explained to Love, "That is all I know."

Love knew what the wind was whispering about, the rainbow bubble outside the seed would get very thin on the last day and just before it would pop open, the feeling could be seen smiling at her reflection from inside on the seventh day. The same was true for the dark bubble, where the feelings would burst into a cry when they would see their own reflection from inside it. Love was glad that she could control it, since she had only love for everything around her.

Doubt and Envy both approached Pride, but she showed no interest in them. They thought to persuade her, but she was still stubborn. They went to Fear to help persuade Pride and when Fear interfered, Pride resisted yet again, saying that they might think about earning her. Fear agreed and told them to fight for it since the idea of a fight appealed to him.

Envy and Doubt, both were strong feelings and started arguing over who deserved Pride more. Trust was a beloved feeling in the consenzi where Pride was gaining popularity due to her beauty. When Trust saw them argue, he thought to help them solve the issue without fighting. He called three of them to his chambers and asked them to answer his question. Whoever got the answer right would get what he asked in return.

"What is a valuable possession that you are very keen to have and once you have it, you want to share it but the problem is that once you share it, you will no longer possess it?" asked Trust, smiling at them, while they stood with bowed heads.

While Doubt thought about all the insecurities that came into his mind, Envy was thinking about the possessions that others had, and he wanted to get his hands on. They both started mumbling and Doubt found it hard to stay there, as he did not believe Trust was deciding fairly. His nature dominated him relegate his fate in Trust's hands and he doubted his way out. After Doubt had left, Envy stayed, declaring that only he could partner with Pride, since his nature forbade him to leave without taking what he had desired.

"The real answer to your riddle, is a SECRET," Pride claimed with arrogance, "And since none of them gave the answer right, they both have lost the right to earn me as their partner. Now, I can ask you for anything, since I am the one who got it right."

"I thought they were the ones who wanted to win you if they answered correct," said Trust, "But, I guess you are right and as I said, the one who answers right shall get what he or she desires. So, what is it that you desire?"

"I want to plant my seed in the green mountains with the consenzis, not amongst those who serve here," exclaimed Pride.

Trust was surprised, for no such claim had been made before, but he was bound by his word and he told Pride that he would request Love to honor her wish.

Trust asked Love to grant Pride to partner with the consenzi, but Love did not agree, for she was reminded of the prophecy. Love had so much love to offer that she agreed to let Pride dwell in the mountains like the consenzis, but she could not allow a collusion.

Trust was bound for his word and Pride held him accountable to it. The day of the festival was approaching, and Trust was down with the promise he had made to Pride. Passion had told Trust before that she wanted to plant a seed with him on the festival, but she could not bear seeing Trust go through a bad time. He told Passion that he would not be able to give his hundred percent to the nourishing of the seed, because not keeping his word was troubling him. Passion wanted to help, so she told him that she would help him keep his word, all he had to do was to keep his trust in her. Passion took Pride along with them a day before the festival to collect a seed from the land lying between the mountain and the dark valley. Then, she told Trust and Pride to stay together with it till dawn and name the fruit of their bond.

The next day, nature was in highest bloom. The sun, wind, and the land presented their best appearance to cherish the seeds of the feelings that wanted to plant their bonds in the soil. Love floated ahead and stood in front of the feelings beside the tree of nature, where she gestured the feelings to come forward with what they had.

"We bring our Hope, which will be an aspiration for everything good that is to come. Help us to nourish this together and bring positive expectations to this land." Compassion and Kindness came forward with the seed of Hope.

"We bring our Blessed seed to this land with love and care. Help us to nourish it with purity and serenity," Purity and Serenity brought the seed Blessed.

While standing low in the dark valley, Doubt and Shame put forth the seed of Hate; that would add to the dislike and guilt prevailing in the valley. Grief and Depression brought out their seed of Despair.

At the mountain top, Trust and Passion came forward with their seed, with Pride standing along with them.

"We want to plant the seed with a little apprehension, because we were not able to decide a name for it," Trust stepped forward with the seed.

"Then, maybe you can wait another year," said Love.

"No, we have cherished this seed and trust me, Love, that it shall bring uniqueness to this land," said Trust. Trust and Pride could not find a common name, so they thought to decide it once the seed took its creative form.

"Fine then, proceed with the planting," Love told them, while she watched all feelings bring forth the seeds of their bond.

Love rose above and raised her hands high as the winds gathered to blow, the sun was shone brightly, and clouds began to gather. All the feelings bearing the seeds came forward and buried their seeds near the tree. Love's hands were raised, and small drops of rain started to pour on the soil. Envy was watching Pride keenly for he still desired her. He could see that just before burying the seed, Pride took Trust's hand and Passion just stood by his side to cover her partner. Pride and Trust planted the seed with the help of Passion.

It rained lightly for seven days while the sun was shining too, and the wind blew softly. Trust nourished the seed with belief and trust, so it had a strong confidence when it came out and Pride nourished the seed with all the narcissism and vanity that it had. Passion gave it self-love to nurture.

The night before the seventh day, the rain got heavy and a bolt of lightning struck the skies. There had never been a storm before and anytime something different happened, Love would think about the prophecy. She had so much love to offer to her fellows that she wouldn't tell anyone, for she did not want others to worry about the balance of this land.

Chapter 9

As the day arrived, Love went early to bless the feelings before their bubbles popped to reveal them. Hope and Blessed smiled on their reflections before they came out, while Despair and Hate gave out a cry of sorrow before coming out. The fruit of Trust and Pride took some time and Love stood there, keenly watching it, but just before coming out, it smiled upon its reflection and Love was more than happy to welcome them all.

It did come as a surprise that the new individual had very different hair that were never seen before, but all the feelings had different skin tones, so they thought it was just a unique color of the hair. She was magnificent and fair with hair brighter than the sun. Everyone stared at it in awe. Love was relieved after seeing that it had smiled at her reflection. It was so unique that they took some time and called it Ego, a unique name that no one had ever heard before.

All the feelings rejoiced and dwelled in the land, with Peace keeping the balance where Trust taught Ego to have more conviction in himself, Pride taught it more about being self-involved. When Passion would approach Ego, Pride made sure to interfere by making Ego realize that pride mattered more than passion. Ego was gaining power with two consenzis and an ugowen helping it to grow. Ego had a very strong consenzi with a tint of ugowen. It was soon being said that Ego had the magnificence of Love and a strong sensation. When feelings were near Ego, they would be affected by it, just like they were affected by Love.

As the feelings were increasing in number, Love told Fear to manage them into groups, each headed by a consenzi. Trust managed Envy, Loyalty and Betrayal. Passion was told to manage Vanity, Self-love and Pride. Pride mumbled to Ego that she wished to be in charge, but still she was considered as one of the servers.

"Why don't you ask them who would like to be in charge?" Ego came forward, feeling for her nurturer.

Everyone stood there in silence, for no one had ever dared to speak after Love had decided something.

"We don't have to ask them as it is important to keep the balance here in check, by prioritizing consenzi over ugowen," said Love, with a smile.

"I would say that it is not fair, just because you belong to the consenzi. What if you were from the ugowen, you would want to be given priority too." Ego stood high, with his voice getting louder.

"I love you all, but the truth is that the negative needs to be checked or else one cannot escape a downfall," explained Love, standing taller.

"So, everyone should adjust their life here according to everything that has been laid out for them. I don't believe in that and I most certainly do not believe in following the rules that I am forced to follow." Ego stood against Love, eye to eye. They both had a strong consenzi and no one dared to interfere. They were witnessing what had never happened in so many years.

"As long as I can, I will keep the balance with love, because that is the only way one can cherish one's time on this land." Love had a strong voice, still exuberating love.

"Then I refuse to stay here, I am fine with myself and I can grow without you nurturing me. I have the right to live by my own rules." Ego stared into her eyes before leaving. They all gasped and none had the courage to speak against two strong consenzis.

Ego left, and started dwelling on the land between the mountains and the dark valley. Everyone spoke of how Ego stood against Love, some sided with Ego, while others showed loyalty to Love.

"Why don't you let me be the head of our group?" Envy asked Trust.

"I have never gone against Love and I cannot. I am her trust."

"Are you sure you have never done anything to betray that, because I know where Ego gets his negativity from. I know you colluded with Pride."

Trust was surprised that Envy knew about the collusion, "I had given my word to Pride and Passion helped me do that."

"You really think that the only reason Pride colluded with you was to be amongst the consenzis?"

"Yes, I do, and I had promised to help her."

"Then you really are easy at trusting others too, because she made a promise to Fear and now, she is fulfilling that."

"Why are you telling me this now?"

"I wanted her before, but now I want more than just Pride, I want you to plead to Love to make me in charge here," Envy threatened Trust, though ugowens had always served the consenzis and kept a low image in obedience, but things were changing after Ego stood up against Love. Ugowens were changing their tones.

Trust pleaded with Love, but Love resisted, comforting every feeling, that they must realize that she could not allow a shakedown of the balance. Instead, she told Trust to use his consenzi to convince his fruit of Ego and bring Harmony. She had been warned by the nature to keep the balance in check and now she was more than ever bent on keeping it, for she did not want to be the cause of their downfall. But Love seemed to be getting weak as the feelings were going against her orders, ugowens wanted to be given priority, so they stopped coming to serve the consenzis. Love tried to make amends, but ugowens wanted to be given preference.

Trust found Ego building a home on the land between the mountain and the valley. Trust was told by Love to persuade Ego to choose a feeling and come to the festival bearing the seed. Love thought that maybe this way, Ego would learn to make peace with the consenzis.

"I do not like to follow your rules because what I do is right, and I feel like a prisoner on that mountain. I don't belong there, where everyone is trying to please each other."

"You don't have to come back. Just come to the festival to ensure unity for our sake, for the sake of the man who helped to nurture you. Please, do it for me, if you don't care about the land or its rules, you must care about the person who brought you here."

"Fine, I will, you don't need to blackmail me. I will bring whoever I want to, there will be no conditions to that."

Trust did not want to betray Love again, he persuaded Grace to ask Ego to partner with her, but Ego turned her down, knowing that she was sent by Trust. Passion persuaded Ego to be there too.

The day before the festival, all the feelings gathered near the tree to collect seeds and choose the best one. Love halted above, standing near the tree, praying to nature to bless all the feelings. There was silence and everyone stood still. Love turned around to see Ego standing up close.

"I am glad you came to take part." Love smiled at Ego.

"On one condition, that you will let me choose who ever I want," Ego said loudly, "I want you to declare to everyone that you will shower it with all the love that you can give, while I plant it on the land in between these two. I want to have my own place of feelings."

"I promise that," Love resisted, as she remembered the prophecy, but Ego had come to her in front of everyone and now he demanded her promise in front of all the feelings that looked to her love. She needed to keep peace and she assured herself that it was not likely for a feeling to go for its opposite. "I will give my blessings to whoever you choose. I promise, for I want love and peace here."

"Then I choose Fear, and I want Love to bless my seed every day, while we nurture it," Ego said loudly.

"Fear is a feeling of the highest ugowen and –"

"And I have the word of the highest consenzi that she will nurture that seed," Ego interrupted Love.

Love nodded, unable to say much with all the ugowens looking at her, "I love you all, and I want you all to flourish, despite your likes or dislikes."

Love stayed longer there by the tree after everyone had left. She didn't know what to do, so she went to meet Ego and tell him about the prophecy. She would beg Ego with every pint of love in her, not to be stubborn. When Love arrived at her house, she was surprised to see that Ego was covering the inside of her walls with glass mirrors. Ego turned away after fixing a mirror amongst the rest, making one wall complete.

"I didn't hope to see you here," she said, as she turned back from the last piece that completed the giant mirror wall.

"You surely like looking at your reflection," Love told her and as she saw her reflection in the mirror, it was nothing like what Ego was in appearance.

"Your refection?" Love's lips stuttered, as she pointed to it. "Your reflection is different." Some trembling words came out while her hand paused in the air.

"What are you talking about? I am more beautiful in my reflection and I want my house to be filled with mirrors so I can look at myself as much as I want," Ego flaunted, as she always did while talking about her beautiful appearance.

Ego reflected self-obsession that was appealing to itself but at the same time, repulsive to others, so its reflection appeared hideous to the other person. That was the moment when Love realized that Ego was not a pure feeling, it was a state of being with a combination of both, the consenzi and the ugowen. The words of the prophecy echoed through her head, "It will not be a pure feeling and you will not be able to stop it, you may find ways to fix it, but it will happen under your command." The impact of this shock had knocked her out of her senses, and she struggled to say something.

"Did you come here to tell me something after you have given your word to me in front of everyone?" Ego was looking at her in a surprise, as Love stood there, stunned with the echo bouncing in her head. It had been a few years and how quickly was her trust betrayed by her own and she just felt the sharp knife that had been stabbed in her back. She had been the warmth of sunshine, the source of light, and the wind of love to all that she cherished, yet it wasn't long till she was betrayed by her very own.

"Are you alright?" Ego could see that Love was not herself and she was turning to leave.

Love stared at Ego's ugly reflection once again, and realized that Ego was more than a feeling, it was an ugly impact that was pleasant to itself but ugly to those who did not possess it. Ego was charming to her own eyes, Love remembered how it had smiled before the bubble of its own self-image had popped to reveal it, but Ego had found a way to be popular with its manipulative nature. For it understood both, the good and the bad.

Love's passion for her feelings had resulted in this blind trust. Trust could always seek Love for help, yet it chose to betray it with Pride. Trembling with the agony of betrayal, she left to seek nature's help.

"You can be careful, but the prophecies come true, you know," the wind whispered to Love, "You focus on stopping, yet you should always aim for solving it once it does happen." The wind cloud was fading away, "Go ahead and nurture the seed of both, dark and light, so that you can save it from doom. Give a touch of your love to the fruit of Ego, that is a product of betrayal."

Love thought she could undo it, but it had already been done. Ego was at its peak and all the feelings were divided, Love could not risk a fight. What united them was the seed festival that she had to bless. So, Love took an oath with nature to bring love and light into the seed of the dark.

All through the seven days, Love blessed the seed of Ego and Fear planted on the land. Love had never cherished a seed like that before for seven days. All the feelings were dividing further now, seeing that Love had favored this seed of Power, a name that Ego had given to it.

It was an amazing day when Power came into life, he had the face of Ego, the attitude of Fear, and the spirit of Love. Power seemed more manipulative than Ego or Fear combined. Power seemed to threaten every other feelings' existence at the same time, captivating them by its essence. The moment Power was born, all the feelings approached it with the purpose of being close to it.

Power nourished under Ego, with Fear intruding in to give it the sustenance of insecurities. Love would give it the extra attention whenever it could. After Ego, the feelings had started staying in their own lands, but after Power joined Ego, all the feelings seemed to be in the fight to gaining Power. Love was pure and wanted to save the land for the love of her fellows. Yet, all the feelings considered that Love too was corrupted by Power, because it showered her love on Power. Love was pure with the utmost consenzi that seemed to be getting weak now.

A war initiated, where desire for Power got stronger and Love felt weaker with every passing day. The land was losing its color, and the feelings lost their spirit, they all wanted to be with Power. Love in its weakness called out to nature once again.

"It has already been done, my Love," the cloud of wind was darker than ever, "We warned you that there would be consequences when you asked for a partner. You cannot expect different feelings and emotions to live in harmony. Different attitudes never unite under love; they always want to go their own way." Wind came closer to Love, for she had tears in her eyes. It was the first time that Love cried, asking nature to save them before her race ceased to exist. The place near the tree where her tear fell became damp and wind came closer to hug Love.

"I am asking you to help me," cried Love, "I am your pure child, the seed of your spirit, help me save my race and I shall never ask for anything more."

"Take Power to be your partner and sow the seed of your bond, only then will you be able to save your fellows." The nature once again took a pity on Love, "All the feelings want to attain Power, if the ugowens win, then the doom shall wipe you all from this land, but if you are able to save them by bonding with their most desired state, then the fruit of Love and Power will be strong enough to take you to a world where you can survive."

"This land is corrupted with Power and the feelings no more respond to Love. How can I make Power listen to me?" Love cried to nature.

"Power has the spirit to collude with Love and form an ultimate power. Find a way, or else we will not be able to save you."

Love spent the whole night sitting near the tree. All the feelings relied on each other and in order to survive, they bonded and planted a fruit of their union. They all tried to seek the best option for them, and Love was the ultimate and highest bond. She went to Power to present itself and Power told her that others would not agree to this mighty union because they all wanted to attain Power for them. When all the rest were busy in their fight to attain Power, Love pursued Trust to help her.

"I know that like every other feeling, you seek Power too, but remember that you have betrayed me once by keeping your word to the ugowens." Love confronted Trust for the betrayal and told him that he was responsible for this chaos. Trust pleaded for a chance to be trusted again. Love told him about the prophecy and asked Trust to help her. "If you want to regain your place with me, then help me persuade Power."

True power could not survive without Trust and Trust was there to help them, even though all the feelings were against it. Power sneaked out with the help of Trust and joined Love; they buried the seed where the soil was still damp with Love's tears. When the word spread that Power had colluded with Love, the ugowens were outraged, they floated across the land to fight for Power.

The wind covered the seed with a cloud of trust, the soil held on to it with power, and the sun radiated it with love for seven days. After seven days, the fruit of Love and Power emerged to astonish everyone. It overpowered every other feeling, including Ego. Its aura was strong enough to make them all bow down in obedience. The second it emerged from the bubble, the fights stopped, and everyone surrendered to its presence. The land was damaged after the seven days of fighting. Fear had swept across the consenzis with force, while the only thing holding them at serenity was the touch of love.

Love rejoiced in happiness and embraced her fruit, calling it Awareness. All in pure white, radiating the energy of the nature, Awareness took over the rest. It guided them to follow it to a land that was owned by a species that were superior to everything else.

A land where humans lived in lostness and were unaware of their true power. The feelings would feed there on the human emotions and live in their subconscious. They would serve as guide to the humans to seek the purpose of their lives. The humans seek their ultimate truth and it shall be brought to them by Awareness.

Awareness lead the feelings and they all followed her in obedience. They have been dwelling alongside the humans in their subconscious, they feast on human thoughts and emotions to keep them alive.

Amour poured another cup of tea and reclined in his chair.

"That was a long tale to walk you through," he smiled at me, "I hope you are not tired."

"Not at all," I put my cup forward for more tea, "In fact, I am so excited that I chose to embark on this journey. So, if Awareness is there, feelings co-exist to keep balance?"

"Awareness helps the humans understand their realities through wisdom and knowledge." Amour put his cup on the side, "It's been many years and the feelings have multiplied many times since then. All of them surrender to Awareness, which is visible through human consciousness. Consciousness and knowledge are offered by Awareness to only those who seek to find the truth."

"Will I find what I seek?"

"It is not a one-day solution and definitely not up to us. In your subconscious, you go through a series of tests, just like you do in your conscious life, to overcome your feelings and fight negative thoughts in order to be more conscious. Once you learn to attain more consciousness, you will have power over every negative hurdle in your life."

"Am I a consella or an ugnaster? Can we know when we are ready?"

"Have you seen that sometimes, you meet people who have a personality that lasts, they have a satisfaction about life and an aura of positivity around them because they learn to attain higher energy? They are surrounded by the feelings of Love." Amour leaned forward as he talked intensely, "And there are some people who have so much discontent in life that they leave a negative mark around them. If you meet such people, they can bring you down because they are surrounded by the feelings of Fear.

Consellas have such strong personalities that they can lift your moods and make their mark, while Ugnasters have such low energy that can affect you in feeling bad about life."

"What about Ego and Power?"

"Didn't you learn, that ego and power are not pure feelings? They are unique in giving the humans their identities. They have superior energy and collude with feelings." Amour got up to leave, "Awareness helps to go through the series of competitions in your subconscious, with the help of knowledge and wisdom. My job today was to help you understand about the evolution of ego and consciousness. If you want to learn more, practice consciousness every day and bring consenzis in your daily life."

Chapter 10

"Our youth includes the young people who have crossed teenage, they have a span of time where they take a break after children's ministry," Joshua explained, as we followed him to the front isles. "As adults, they face the demons of desire and despair, we show them to come up with strategies to settle their affairs and they figure out how to live on with the right mindset."

We stopped at the congregation where we met an old man whose black skin contrasted with his grey hair. He had a pleasant face and greeted us with a smile.

"This is our minister of education, Desta Akochi," Joshua introduced us to this man, "He was not here in our first meeting, but he manages the youth programs at our church."

"I am very happy to meet you," Akochi greeted us, "Joshua has briefed me about your mission here and I am delighted to see that the spirit of peace exists in the non-church community."

"This mission is a part of our education process, our universities encourage us to make stronger bonds with the people of other religion and countries," said Emre, "A desire to raise better youth is one common factor that unites the education system everywhere."

"I appreciate your spirit and respect your desire," Akochi had a very strong African accent, "Feel like this is your home and you are welcome to address our people. You will see all kinds of color and races here, which itself is a testimony that we make no difference amongst the people of God."

Joshua led us to the front row where we sat with him. I looked around and saw so many different people that I had never seen before. Though it reminded me of my vision of the red book that I had started reading. It seemed like the council of the Wise where they had so many different faces. I took out my diary to take notes. My mind was beginning to be more alert than ever and I could not help thinking about the people sitting there while taking down my notes.

"The role of the youth is to show up and address the pain felt when betrayed by a friend at school."

The role of the youth is to practice vulnerability by sharing the disorientation felt when abandoned by a parent at home," Akochi addressed the youth, "The role of the youth is to put us on the spot by asking the question, 'why?,' when dealing with the death of a loved one. The first step towards evolving in the path of peace is to let your questions out and never let them bother you inside."

The resemblance of so many different people to the feelings of my dream was uncanny, yet it wasn't the skin or hair color that defined them. It is so strange that we have made our outer appearances define who we are but even then, no person can truly be defined on those. Just like the skin or hair color could not define the identity of a feeling. When we focus on the appearances, we are deceived by the reality of what lies within that appearance, for the truth is never too easy to grasp. The truth is never as easy as what we see, it is way beyond the superficial guise. The appearances may be the characteristics of a species or a nation, yet they are never the true identities. I was thinking to myself while trying my best to stay more active in the youth session. The book had a strong impact on me that was making me more aware of my present moments, but the resemblance of this council to the one in my vision was making my mind drift into analyzing life on a different level.

"The Church needs young people. The Church needs its youth to model for adults what it means to be vulnerable, raw, and tender. The Church needs reminders that we are called by our faith to be a community of conviction that is relevant, authentic, and courageously honest," Joshua was talking softly in his African accent, "May God empower all youth to bring the real joys and struggles of their lives to trusted communities of faith so that the Church can experience LOVE in our moments of weakness."

As I sat there hearing about God, I wondered what could be the reason that humans were created with different skin and hair. One claiming to be superior to the other, though there is no proof of superiority being confined to appearances. If our creator had created us with the intention of love, then why would He make us different in appearances that could become a source of dispute in our lives? I wondered, while taking notes, as my mom's words echoed in my ears.

"The blue cover goes over this new album," my mom was wrapping some of her albums with new covers, "I think the pictures of one whole year should have the same tone of color with different shades."

"Why would you want to cover them with different wraps when all they contain are pictures? I mean, you know they are all albums, why make them look different on the outside?" I asked her, while going through some childhood photos.

"I deal with my photo collection like an artist, and artists make sure that every piece of their art is unique." My mom placed the new blue album with the other shades of blue in the book rack. "Have you ever seen a writer write different books with the same book cover or a painter shade all his paintings in the same color?" My mom came close to me, "That's because you want every piece of your work to have a different identity that makes them unique."

I stopped writing and looked around me once again, we were created by one true artist, who made us in different tones, giving us uniqueness. So, we all stand out from each other, we are all blessed with unique identities that define us. That is what a real creator with the love for its work does. A writer wants his book to stand out from the rest of the books but at the same time, he will not make his next piece of work the same as before. Though he has equal love for all his work of creations.

"From the perspective of freedom of religion or belief, the converted prominence of religion in international political life harbors positive opportunities, but may also include some perils," Akochi's address was followed by a lecture from Emre. "On the positive side, it leads to a transformed acknowledgment of the logical implication that religion or belief apparently has for countless people."

This is what a true artist does. It doesn't mean he prefers one work over the other, but it shows his real love and passion for his own creation. The same was true for the feelings from my vision, they were the works of nature and nature is all about creating art. A piece of art is unique in its own way, the creator shows his love by making it different and not the same as the rest. The humans stand out from the rest of the creation, they are superior in reasoning. At the same time, each human is distinguished from the other because each one of us has a unique outlook that gives us our identity. Some make the most of it by accepting their identities as unique and make the best of what it offers, while others stay in the shadows, not realizing their distinctiveness. This is what the whole high energy was about. I was getting it now. When the energy of our identity is in tune with the good feelings, then we can learn to excel in the world, and we stand among the consellas. The nature has a feeling of peace and a sense of calmness because the energy of the nature is perfect, it acts like a creator for those that grow from it. That is why the first feeling that was purely the intention of nature was Love. The energy of love is in tune and in the same vibration as the energy of nature, and so the more Love we bear, the closer we are to nature and peace.

Racial, religious, or communal type discrimination is a by-product of negative thinking, for we only belong to a certain type because our ancestors happened to be born with it. People are ready to fight or go to war for the beliefs that have been engraved in their minds by their ancestors. There is no other truth to our appearances and beliefs, other than the fact that we happen to be born in families with the likes of it.

"The role of faith or belief cannot be consigned to a mere private domain. For many devotees, it also has a public dimension, which brings it close to policymaking and administration, in the complete consideration of public affairs…" Emre's lecture was generalized and related to making the youth realize their strong impact if they wanted to join politics, as we had promised the church authorities that our job was to make the youth realize their roles in shaping the future and politics of their countries. "…whereas the demands for more religious learning in international politics and peacekeeping are certainly vindicated, they should be associated with a compact understanding of freedom of religion, as an essential part of global human rights decree…"

Knowing that we were U.N. volunteers and we wanted to motivate the youth to take part in creating a better world, no matter which institute they represented, most of the youth became interested in how they could be a part of the U.N. peace program. Some participants questioned if religious human rights exist in the international affairs.

"It might be beneficial to discriminate between a religious basis and a religious obligation of human rights. Human privileges are earthly standards in the sense of not being dependent of any religious reasoning or basis. However, this does not prevent the option to logically validate human rights from a sincere religious perception, which means giving a religious appreciation of human rights, including in doctrinal philosophy. A religious appreciation of human rights is imperative and should be shared from all sides. Our aim is to focus on the issues that bring us together, instead of concentrating our energy on the reasons that divide us…"

Chapter 11

"Nah, not this one," I told Samantha, looking at her new dress.

"What? This is my favorite and it's perfect for a summer party." Samantha looked at her reflection in the mirror.

Her room was so cozy that I could spend the whole day lying in her bed.

"Will you get out of the bed and start getting ready now?" She went to her dressing room to try another outfit.

"Nope, not until you have figured out your dress for the party," I started playing on her tab while still in the bed, "I know that it doesn't take me long to get ready, but I hate waiting for you because you take so long and you are never sure of what to wear. So, I am going to stay in my comfy bed and enjoy my game till you decide what you have to wear."

"How is this one?" Samantha was putting on a long dress with dark stripes, "Will you at least clear up the room before we leave? It's a mess here and please throw away these origamis, they were just for our practice, you never fill your room with these, then why do you mess mine?"

"What are you, a zebra now? Besides, I never ask you to clean up my room, so I won't clean up yours either. I never do origami in my house because my mom doesn't allow it, she has a weird thing about making animals from papers."

"Hey, did you fill out the entry forms? I mean, we are supposed to be joining next month." Samantha was busy yet trying something else, "Can you believe how far we have come? I mean, it just seems like yesterday, when we would go to school and now, we are going to university." Samantha came out in black jeans and a summer top, "I think this is my choice for tonight. And Meryl," she looked away from the mirror, "I am so happy that we are going to the same universities, I couldn't be happier." Samantha was always expressive about her emotions, unlike me.

"Yes, I am happy too." I placed my tab on the side, "I guess I should go to get ready now. I will meet you at the door after half an hour. Please, don't be late."

I got up to leave but heard someone coming upstairs. We both looked at each other, as we thought that Samantha's parents had gone out.

"Oh my, I am not supposed to be going anywhere today. I must finish filling up my forms and mail my documents. My dad will never allow me to go to the party." Samantha was hiding the dresses she had been trying out for the party, "Quickly, hide behind the door, you are not supposed to be here, and I am supposed to be working."

This was not the first time I was hiding in her room and I am pretty sure our parents knew it now, because we had been covering up for each other since we were little kids. I quickly ran behind the door and Samantha was trying to clean up as quickly as she could. There was a knock and Samantha sat down on her desk taking hold of her documents.

"Come in," said Samantha, quickly trying to sound busy as ever.

Her father entered the room with a smile, "Are you done with your forms, my dear? I was on my way to meet a friend and I thought I could help you mail those documents."

"Yes, Dad, I need to mail them soon, but I am still working on them." Samantha pretended to stare at them like she was busy with them from a long time.

"I hope you are not having any trouble writing your essay."

"No, Dad, its fine, I was just trying to make sure I do not make any mistakes. I am sure I will mail them at night."

"Please make sure you do not delay them anymore and mail them by tomorrow. I hope you are able to finish them by the night." Her dad looked around her messy room, "Wow, origami, I didn't know you liked making these."

"It's just something Meryl and I learned from online workshops. We do it for fun to pass our time. It's not a hobby, Dad." Samantha got up from her chair, waiting for her dad to leave so that he wouldn't spot me. "How do you know about origami? You ever made these?"

"No, I didn't." Mr. Remy went towards the window, "But I once knew a woman who loved origami. I don't know about origami, but she was a very special woman."

"Mom has never liked origami, Dad."

"I know, I am talking about someone else, she was a friend, a very special friend." He was looking outside the window, with his broad back facing towards me.

I peeked from the back of the door and saw a broad back facing the window with his hands behind his back and his little finger twitching with pace. I resisted blinking so that I could make out of his face through the sunrays and see where I had seen this image before.

"What happened to her?"

"I can't say, but all I know is that she doesn't work with origami anymore, just a silly bet I made with her."

My brain stammered for a moment and my eyes got wider than ever, every part of me went on a pause while my thoughts fastened up. My mind was blank and my eyes eclectic, as I stared at him in horror.

I saw the shadow of my lamp on the ceiling, my heart was beating fast against my chest, and the impact of my dream was strong enough to make me cry. It was the day of my life that had haunted me for a long time. The remnants of my past still clung onto my mind like creepers on the wall. No matter where I was in my life, it always came back to my life with my mom. I could spend the whole day doing something else and having a new purpose for tomorrow, yet I always woke up with the voices of the past.

I pulled myself up and took the giant book from the side table and gazed at it for some time. The deep, red cover seemed like the color of fresh blood, I wanted to read more and dive into the realms of my subconscious and seek the world beyond the human senses. I opened it and placed my fingertips from where I had left it the last time. I felt the book talking to me once again.

Adrenaline deluges my system; it impels and thumps like it's trying to outflow. I think my heart will shatter and my eyes are wider in search for light. My body wants to run away and seek shelter where I would never have to be in the dark again, but instead, I remain where I am. Unlike the last time, this place has an unease and frightful appeal. I still want to stay and face the challenge that this book offers. I do not wish to be a slave to the shadows of the past or my own fear. I want to be able to fight past them.

I find it hard to see, but at some point, I will have to move beyond this feeling. I pull the courage to move forward and suddenly a flash of light wakes up the room with a loud noise. I feel cold and frightened. Life seems to be draining from my soul and my energy is getting low. I see the woman from the last time I was here. Peur stands tall in the left corner, looking down upon me.

"Don't be frightened, my dear," Peur speaks with a broken voice, "The world is a sad place, it is only through sorrow and pain, that you are able to feel what life really is. There is nothing good about it. Life is short and everything good in it is temporary. So, embrace the pain and sorrow, for they are your real friends. Live in fear and you shall have an eternal friend."

"I do not want a life of horror and fright," I remember that Amour was talking about facing challenges if I wanted to seek peace in my life, "I want to fight and live long enough to know that I never gave up." I muster up all the courage I have, for I do not want to fail.

Peur stands opposite to me now, putting her hands forward in the form of fists, "I take no desire in winning you down. None. It's just compulsory. Taking down the weak is low, even for me, because you are a weakling."

"You love to hurt, and I can't heal myself with you around." My legs are shaking with fear, yet I put on a valiant face, "I have no choice but to face what you put me up to. I am determined to get hold of my life, so then, see me come out fighting." I get scared as I see Peur approaching with hard-made fists.

"I haven't even swung a blow yet, and I see you shudder. How weak you are. This isn't malice, this is pity and justice combined." Peur forces a punch on my chest, "You cannot control yourself and so, I control you. Fight me and you know I'll win, or maybe you like gambling?"

I was surprised by how hard she hit me. Just as I could gain control of myself, I received another blow from her on my right cheek. I quickly grasp her other fist that was about to hit me, "I never came looking for a fight. I am a conciliatory by nature, but no one stands back and takes blows in a fight, unless they are a deficient moron." I raise my hand to punch her back, but she pushes me away and starts punching on my body; heavy, maniacal, smashing punches, heavy as the boom of oaken planks, bullets to the body, bolts to the head.

"You are a weak human, you let go of your family, abandoned your mother when you knew that she needed you. You left her when she begged you to stay." She punches me till I am out of breath. Her punching is so crisp and sharp, it feels like electric jolts, zzt, zzt, zzt, even when they land on my arms.

"I had no choice, I had to go away." I was blocking her heavy blows with all the effort I could put in the fight.

"So that's what you humans tell yourself every time you let someone down, every time you make a mistake, and every time you muster regrets and shame. You are not only scared; you are ashamed of the choices that you made in your life." She kicks a heavy blow into my knee.

A rapid flood of pain jolts throughout my body. My stomach twinges, my arms are losing tension, and my legs begin to wane. "You will not get the better of me," I say, as I drop to the ground. My tongue is tasting blood and I know I must overpower the fear resonating in my subconscious. "For years, I had been grateful to the man who only pretended to be my friend's dad and nothing more. I thought my mom and I owed him. I had spent my whole life living a lie, not knowing that the man responsible for our miseries was right there the whole time." My head is pounding and just as she forces her right fist, I punch her face with all the might, snapping her nose into a grotesquerie. "What was I supposed to do, thank him and my mom for making me lead a life of lie and pretention?" I continued hitting Peur in the face, receiving blows when she got a chance, but I could feel her getting tired.

"Well, as long as you stay in your doubt of whether you did the right or wrong thing, I will stand by you to support your doubts."

"I did all I could to stay positive with them, but how could I, after knowing that they were just a part of the lie that I was living." I keep fighting her blows away with rage.

"Your guilt gives me strength, but your anger is very important to me as well. It can make you feel powerful but that's just temporary because in the long run, anger keeps me burning with desire to bring you down."

"I did what I had to, so I wouldn't have to face the truth." I hit her hard and she kneels down on the floor, "I think I just ran away. I wish to change what I did without letting it hurt anyone. That's it, I was very angry, but I didn't want to hurt anyone." I try to stay in the light because I can see Peur fading into the darker shadow.

I see someone appearing from the right side, "Is that you, Amour?" I ask, feeling a sense of calmness reviving around me.

"I knew you had it in you," Amour approaches me with something shining in his hand, "Sometimes, in order to overcome your negativity, all you have to do is speak about it."

"Did I defeat Fear?" I feel like the fight did not worn me down. There is blood on my knuckles and bruises on my body, yet I can't recall the fight itself.

"Maybe for now," Amour comes closer to me, "But what's more important, is what you learn from every challenge; the things you need to do to attain higher energy."

"I understand now that every feeling is necessary, it's how we deal with them that matters in the long run," I gain my breath back, "I thought Fear had me." Peur had vanished into the dark.

"Fear is a kind of psychosis, but one that is useful if you know how it works. Fear will take you by the hand to the things you keep and guard as precious. Always face fear with courage, understand it, and then let it go. Let these fears wake you up, let them show you the way to your true self, to the brave soul whose love shines like a star. For without fear, love is brighter, stronger, and deeper. When you find yourself, my love, you will be your own master, fully healed, and your last fear will be of your own strength." Amour smiles and puts a chain around my neck, "You have earned it. Keep your lessons with you, for these ugowens may return, mightier than ever."

I was shaken by the sound of my mobile. Emre had messaged me to meet him at the Carette. It was a café near our hotel. I washed up and left to see him as soon as I could.

Chapter 12

"I have amazing memories from this place. I visited this cafe the last time I was in Paris. I was staying close by and came here for a quickie, but was not wowed. Perhaps I was jet-lagged. Then again, the next day, I stopped in to grab a quick sweet treat and hot chocolate after a long, cold, rainy day of sightseeing. I had walked from the Eiffel Tower, across the bridge over the River Sienna, and through Trocadero. Since then, it has become my favorite treat-time café." Emre was waiting for his order as I went through the menu. It was close to closing time when I arrived, so it was easy for table seating, and the staff was delightful. I ordered a cake and the hot chocolate. THE HOT CHOCOLATE… Wow… The best I've ever had in my whole life and in all my travels. Not too sweet, not too bitter, but just right and creamy.

Suddenly I got the craving for hot chocolate and was ready to order, "I think I will order that too."

"Allow me to order in French," Emre told me, "The service in France is always better if you speak their language their way."

There was silence on our table for a while, I was expecting that Emre would talk since he called me here, but he sat in silence, "I never thanked you for the book."

"You shall never have to," Emre smiled at me, "I hope you are doing well, you seemed to be lost today at the conference."

"How do you know?"

"I can always feel; you should know this by now," Emre was giggling, "I hope you didn't have much trouble fighting your past."

"It was very frightful at first, but I managed to defeat it for the time being. I get more scared when thoughts become painful." I take a sip of my hot chocolate. And oh my God, it was amazing. Hot chocolate on a cold evening with macaroon is the best thing that I have ever had in Paris.

"Thoughts of the past and painful memories are in fact a state of the mind, where one wishes the past could be any different."

"That's not possible," I claimed with certainty.

"Then why not forgive and let go, rather cling on till the memories eat you up?"

"You remember we talked about the African immigration and Chris told us the story of a woman who worked for a French man," I said in a low voice.

"Yes, of course."

"Well, they moved to Canada, bearing the child of the man she worked for," I say secretively, "And that child is right here sitting in front of you."

Emre sat in silence, fixing his gaze on my face. He didn't say anything and looked down.

"I had never thought that I would be telling you this because I never talk about it," I broke the silence.

"That means you have learnt not to be ashamed of anything that was not your fault."

"It was not my fault, but I did feel guilty for leaving my mother, at the same time trying to cover my anger for her." I was twisting the napkin in my fingers, "I came back running in anger after I found out. My grandfather was going through some of our albums in his study. I asked him directly if Samantha's father was the man my mom met in France, and he was quiet. He told me not to ask my mom. He made me promise that it would hurt her if she found out that she could not protect me like she wanted to. They needed money and support and Remy did not leave them in France when situation got worse. They owed him and he never abandoned them ever since. I was still mad at my mom. I never said anything to her, in fact, I got very quiet and decided to study away from home. She was sad to see me go but I did not let her find out why. She has been trying to get in touch with me for the last seven years, but I never respond. I don't bother replying to her messages, yet she tells me how much she misses me and wishes to see me.

Maybe my guilt came from that, but my anger justified what I had done."

"You are not your pain or your past, you are the soulful being who is superior to all that," Emre assured me, "I am glad you were able to defeat these feelings by just accepting that they exist. The more you run away, the more fear and Ugowens overpower you. Just sharing them is the first step towards evolving into the higher energy."

"I have never even talked about it and just speaking about them makes me feel like it's okay to have had a bad experience." I take another sip of the amazing hot chocolate.

"We cling on to feelings without even realizing them and that is why I said, one reason for that, is a wish that it could have been any different but that's inevitable. What is done cannot be undone and no matter how big the pain, once you learn that it's okay to be disturbed by negative experiences, you are no longer under their control. This way, you are able to talk about them which is the first step towards peace."

I couldn't believe myself. I was talking about things that had been mustered up for years, but here I was, doing the impossible.

"Tell me more about your life if you feel like sharing it now."

It felt like a wonderful evening, we both ordered more hot chocolate and macaroon. I went on talking and we both laughed about the things that I never thought I would be sharing with anyone, let alone my boss.

Chapter 13

The next day, we came to Le Pure, a classic Parisian corner café. It was a charming spot to drop into for a morning coffee, aperitif, contemporary bistro meal, or Sunday brunch. It was such a fun and lively atmosphere, with many locals enjoying their morning drinks and having a good chat. We were all enjoying the bright spring sun that could betray its cheerers anytime.

"I always get a table outside here, the view is charming enough to lighten your day," Chris was leaning on his chair and looking around.

"We are all familiar with the beautiful scenery in Paris, except for Meryl," Jean looked at me, "You should take a walk around these antique shops and then stop over for snacks and coffee sometime. You will really enjoy it. Get out of that hotel of yours."

"Yes, I do, whenever I can find the time," I knew they all talked about Paris and many other pleasures offered by it that I was not familiar with, "In fact, I do enjoy being in a company who knows so much about this place, though it's my first time here, it feels familiar now."

"I see a lot of positivity today," Jean's French accent was very charming, *"Bein pour vous."* He raised his glass to me.

"The first times in traveling are the most memorable," Chris raised his glass too.

"It's lovely in Spring," Emre talked less when we talked about the daily life, he was more about business and his job, "Speaking of Spring in Paris, we have to attend the St. Patrick's Day, not as U.N. officials, but as members of the church that is under our study. Paris will hold its first official St. Patrick's Day discussion forum that will be presided over by the head of the National Front."

"The church youth will be supporting their cause for peace by singing at the Irish Cultural Center," Chris gave his facts, "The Centre Cultural Irlandais has been dedicated to the promotion of Irish artistic creation in France since its inauguration in 2002. Each year, the center hosts an array of cultural festivities in honor of St. Patrick."

"Paris has plenty on offer to ensure you have a *Lá Fhéile Phádraig*," Andrea nodded with pride.

"So, will we be a part of the discussion forum representing the church?" I asked in surprise.

"We started the lectures at the church to be included as part of the youth program, we have information that some activists from the church have planned an attack on the head of the National Front, while supporting them through choir," Emre told us in a low voice. "This is one reason that the secret service wanted us to be a part of the discussion forum."

"So, we are here to investigate too?" Andrea asked Emre.

"Actually, we are here to report anything we find suspicious, at the same time, spreading the message of peace. We serve the U.N. to support peace and watch out for any activities that might disrupt the peace," Emre made it clear to us that we must be on the lookout too while working as peace promoting professors, "Two secret service agents will be standing amongst the security guards for the security of the National Assembly leader. If you suspect anything, you notify them." Emre took out two pictures to help us identify them.

"How would you identify them?" I asked.

"I have my own way," Emre smiled towards me.

"Why would they want to hurt the leader of the National Front?"

"The ministry of the church is said to have ties with the Algerian group, whose families were torn apart in the Paris massacre of 1961. They still haven't forgiven the French authorities. It might be a rumor, but some inside information was given that St Patrick's Day might provide them a chance for vengeance," Emre explained it to us, "As it is all based on a suspicious threat letter, we cannot warn the authorities without proof."

"The events leading up to the tragic night of 1961 were set against a backdrop of rising tensions in France, as it struggled to accept that it was fighting a losing battle to suppress a seven-year struggle for independence in Algeria. In Paris, violence flared between French security forces and FLN members in the months leading up to the October 17 protests. The tipping point was an attack which left several Parisian police officers dead. An incensed Maurice Papon was determined to hunt down the perpetrators and crush all signs of rebellion. One of the measures introduced, was an evening curfew imposed solely on the Algerian community in the Paris city area," Chris gave us the historical facts.

"What is the FLN?" I asked, getting my facts for the draft.

"Front de libération nationale; FLN is a national political party in Algeria. It was the principal nationalist movement during the Algerian war and the sole legal and the ruling political party of the Algerian state, until other parties were legalized in 1989," Jean told me.

"In response, the FLN called on the Algerian community to join non-violent protests in Paris on 17th October. Thousands crammed to landmark sites such as the Saint Michel Bridge near Notre-Dame, the Opéra, Place de la Concorde, and even the Champs-Elysée. The French police attacked the demonstrations under orders from Papon and many Algerians were massacred," Chris continued with his facts.

"Then, as quickly as it happened, the incident was forgotten and in the years that followed, Papon continued to serve the French government in a variety of roles. People were outraged and could not forget the incident for years, while it was being suppressed in the media."

"Did the government do something to reform its ties?" I asked again.

"The Evian Accords included a treaty that was signed on 18th March 1962, in Evian Les Bains France, with the provincial government of the Algerian Republic, the government-in-exile of FLN, which sought Algeria's independence from France with a formal ceasefire and formalized the idea of cooperative exchange between the two countries. After that, the party purged internal dissent and ruled Algeria as a one-party state," Emre added to what Chris was saying, "Many still carried on this rage and vengeance in their hearts for years after 1961, and we got an anonymous letter declaring that the memories of the innocent murders that were long forgotten shall be avenged."

"Wow, the history does teach us a lot if we care to learn," I said, after hearing these sad turnouts, "A second bloodshed to avenge the first one can only lead to a third one."

"But everything is based on a suspicion letter, we can't do much," Jean gave his concern.

"The secret service of U.N. is established as an investigative unit within the Department of Peace. Reporting threats is kind of our part-time job as Peace

Volunteers. Though a threat has been reported based on an anonymous letter, we still have no proof or basis for our precautions," Emre made sure to remind us of the purpose of SUNs every time we had our meetings.

"I feel like every time we meet, I have so much more to learn and at the same time, I am more excited about living a life to do better for this world," I said with a smile.

"Do we have anything more to discuss, because I am getting late for my art exhibition," Jean was getting ready to leave.

"There was not much to discuss, just the fact that we need to be on the lookout, especially when some activity is suspected on the St. Patrick's. We are doing our part as the peace makers, now we will be on the alert for any terrorist activity," Chris gave him a thumbs up.

After Jean left us, Chris went to take a restroom break. Emre took out something from his bag.

"I was thinking that maybe you would like to join me on my visit to Canada, I shall return before our conference here," Emre took out an envelope and placed it in front of me.

"What's this?" I asked in wonder.

"It's a ticket to join me on my trip, if you feel like," said Emre, "I thought maybe you would like to visit someone there."

"How could you?" I said abruptly, "I didn't tell you all those things so that you would plan something like this for me at your own."

"I am just looking out for the people who work for me and most importantly, someone who asked me for help."

"You might be my boss at job, but you are not the boss of my life." I was angry at him, "This is the reason I don't tell people about my personal life because they have nothing better to do than offer solutions."

"I was only trying to help."

"Maybe you could have helped by just listening like a true friend."

"Look, you don't have to go if you don't want," Emre was getting up to leave, "But just give it a thought when you are a bit cool. Remember that when you seek help, you leave it to the other person instead of dictating to be helped your way."

Emre left me alone on the table, and I sat there alone, feeling low about why he would try to interfere.

Chris came back and sat with me, "I have ordered the best thing that you will ever taste here."

"I am sorry, Chris; I am not in the mood."

"Don't tell me you are going to leave too now," Chris asked me to stay, "I didn't have my breakfast. Please try this with me and you will admit that it is the best macaroons you have ever tasted."

I nodded, but stayed quiet. Chris looked at the envelope on the table.

"I am going to tell you something that will make you feel better," Chris carried on without my consent, "I started having problems in my married life because I couldn't tell my wife about the secret mission of U.N. She would ask questions and I couldn't say because I had signed a contract to keep threats a secret. I couldn't focus, so I went to Emre saying that I was ready to give up, but he didn't let me. He told me to tell his wife and take her in confidence. He promised me that if I faced any problem, he would help me. So, I told my wife with a little proof from Emre. He helped me keep a job that I love, at the same time, balance my personal life, my job is my passion, so he didn't let me leave my passion. All I did was go to him with a personal problem."

I was looking at Chris and listening intently.

"I never told you that I did a background check for you when I was your supervisor in New York."

"I didn't know that," I looked in amazement.

"I thought you were the perfect U.N. peace supporter and when they asked me that they were looking for one more person who could help us with analyzing the discussion data and report our progress, I thought of you. I mean, you did such an amazing job working for me." Chris offered me some macaroons that arrived at our table, "I couldn't think of anyone better suited for a job that required dedication."

"Thank you, Chris," I took the macaroons and ordered some hot chocolate with them.

"Not yet," Chris said quickly, "But I did mention to them that you were someone who looked like she was running away from her family. I said that your personal life was in a mess. I was familiar with your parent's history of immigration and you had filed your dad as dead. I told them that there was a clash, either you did not accept, or you did not acknowledge the man who helped your mom without you knowing."

I was shaken by the fact that they already knew so much about me, though I pretended to keep my personal life a secret.

"While I showed our selection board that your personal life was not as polished as your job skills, Emre sided with you for the reason that the personal confusion could be improved, as long as your skills were right for the job." Chris had left his food to talk intently to me, "You see, that's what Emre does, he believes in helping people improve, even if they don't know that they need to. He doesn't let anyone give up when he knows they have the skills to do better."

Chris was right, he had lightened my mood. I did feel like I was overreacting, after all, I was the one who had asked Emre for guidance.

"I have nothing planned for the day, let's take a walk along these shops," Chris told me, "It's too lovely a day to be wasted in a hotel room."

"I hope you are not keeping an eye on me now or secretly keeping a check on me," I smirked.

"You never know." We both laughed and left to take a walk on this pleasant day.

It was one of the most dynamic, ethnically diverse, and trendiest quarters in Paris. Its boulevards and avenues spanned out from Place de la République in the west, to Bastille in the east. Divided into distinct parts, this large chunk of the city contained various neighborhoods that retained their own special atmosphere and associations.

This arrondissement was probably one of the most happening parts of the town with a whole host of restaurants, boutiques, and trendy restaurants to keep any hipster busy. We started exploring the area by walking up Rue Oberkampf and got a feel for the Bohemian atmosphere.

As the name implied, the Bastille area was the location of the Storming of Bastille, which kick-started the French Revolution on July 14th, 1789. Hundreds of years later, this area of the city was still full of spirit, just not the revolutionary kind.

When we got tired of the noise and pace of the city, we took a walk along Canal St. Martin that cured us of the claustrophobia of the city center, and the fact that we spotted Meryl Streep at the Cimetière du Père Lachaise added a twist to my day. I went to take a picture with her but quickly left her in peace.

We then took a stroll in the area around Rue du Marché Popincourt and Rue Neuve Popincourt.

Chris took me to witness the best views of the city from the Parc de Belleville. Although not technically in the 11th, it was also a close walk to Père Lachaise cemetery, the world's most visited and the Paris's largest cemetery.

Named after a confessor of Louis XIV, Père Lachaise was opened in 1804 and now has about 800,000 permanent tenants. The most star-studded cemetery ever, it boasts Chopin, Molière, Proust, Colette, Oscar Wilde, and Jim Morrison amongst its guests.

After Père Lachaise, it was time to eat. There were some great restaurants in the area to choose from.

"Paris Hanoi offers fresh Vietnamese food for lunch. If you are looking for something a little bit more French, then the Café de l'Industrie near Bastille is perfect for a long lunch over a sneaky carafe of red wine." Chris looked towards me.

"Red wine sounds good now."

"French it is."

The old-world décor of the restaurant was bound to charm us and we had an amazing time there, forgetting anything that might have upset me before.

Chapter 14

Even if we are not aware of our emotions right now, they are always being cast inside. The energy that flows through our energy system never stops, and our energy system never stops functioning. We are always radiating energy, whether high or low. I was sitting in the park and wondering at how the energy around each of us was affected by our feelings and emotions.

Each emotion has different characteristics. Anger disappears more quickly than jealousy. The need for revenge is more persistent than jealousy. Some emotions come more frequently than others, and some stay longer than others. This flow of emotions is like a shower. There was a woman in the park who was angry at a man for bumping into her while running. The woman radiated anger and the man was apologetic, but the woman left in anger. She went near her son and scolded him for leaving her sister behind. The boy took his sister and pushed another boy to the floor, seeing that no one was looking. The woman carried the emotion of anger for a long time, while the man who had apologized had joined his friend on the bench and was cheerful. Some emotions like anger are stronger than others, like remorse. The stronger feelings have the ability to pass on to others, they carry more inertia, and are passed onto another person.

The flow of our emotions continues, until the physical body that is the host of these feelings, ceases to exist. It is a flow that never stops, whether we pay attention to it or not. We may dream for a while, but those dreams too are affected by these emotions. I had been away from my family for a long time, yet my feelings and emotions had taken shelter in my body forever. They pinched me from time to time, and not a single night passes without me dreaming about these feelings.

Our emotions always return too. Each time, they show us where and how energy is being processed in our energy system. When we understand that system, we will know why we are experiencing an emotion and how we can change it, if you want to change it.

We do think that others are like us in their thinking pattern, but we all differ in our own way of experiencing energy. Our energy systems are like fingerprints that identify our uniqueness.

We may become angry easily, another person may become frightened, and yet another may become jealous. I remember my grandfather used to shout whenever he was angry. Some people let out emotions and feelings louder than others. I tend to become quiet and shrink into my shell when I am angry. My mom wanted company to feel safe.

Samantha talked all the time, she felt the need to talk, sometimes she would tell me about how her mom left her dad when she was little, but then she went back because Samantha would follow any man to find her dad. She just talked and talked. Some people, like me, tend to stay quiet. I would stay quiet because I never wanted to do the effort of making more friends. It seemed like an effort to talk to people or listen to their stories. I was comfortable with whoever I had in my family; I didn't want to make more efforts.

My mom always feared being alone. She would seek company, even if someone made her angry, she withdrew in the fear of being confronted or left alone by that person. I believe we not only have energy circles, there is a unique quality to each one of those. Some people withdraw and become silent. Some people are frightened to be alone. They need to be in the company of others to feel safe. Some people are frightened when they are with others.

The book had made me realize that when we become aware of our emotions, we are more consciously aware. The more we acknowledge why we are feeling them, the less power they have over us. The moment I realized why I left my home or why I was feeling guilty about it, I felt like I had freed myself from that emotion. Everyone has the same kind of feelings in their subconscious, but we all experience them in a different way.

Every painful emotion brings a different experience for each one of us. When we are angry or jealous, we stand with the Ugowens. When we have doubts and feelings of regrets, we are with Ugowens, but with different experiences. Not every experience in anger is the same and not every experience in jealousy is the same. Becoming emotionally withdrawn when you are angry is one experience, and becoming louder is another. Similarly, every consenzi comes with a different experience.

In fact, we all possess two major energy systems; anger, vengefulness, sadness, and greed are feelings experienced through fear. Joy and gratitude are experienced through love. When we begin to see our experiences this way, all the circumstances that we encounter in our life become meaningful.

We begin to examine them all as experiences that are perfect for bringing our attention to inner dynamics that we might need to change. These could be our painful emotions. Our emotions become the focus of our attention, not the people or circumstances that appear to be creating these feelings for us. Instead of being angry and trying to change circumstances or people, we feel the need to observe our emotions.

My body had experienced these emotions eight years back, yet I feel its effects. An event brings a sense of anger or joy, and our body keeps absorbing these feelings, so we can recall them anytime. Different feelings are associated with different memories. We develop a pattern of acting the same way towards a similar event. I was angry at my dad for leaving, so I kept those feelings to me and avoided talking about them all through my childhood, I couldn't confront my dad or my mom for the lies that they had made me live, so I kept quiet and ever since then, I have stayed quiet for any Ugowens that possessed me. These emotions come from inside of us, not from outside. The times, places, people, and circumstances change, but our anger does not. Nor does our sadness, vengefulness, or fear.

I cannot change all the people that make me angry, jealous, or sad, but I can change myself. How others act or speak is not as important as how I respond to them, because my body will absorb that as feelings and my experience will depend on my response. It is like changing your reflection, which is impossible, the feelings smiled or cried because of what they reflected into the bubble.

My body is like a house that receives different guests in the form of feelings. Every morning is a new morning, but why is it that every morning I get up, my mind starts chattering about something that happened years back. I might have left people behind, but my mind still talks to them when they are not around. I want to seek happiness in life and pursue my dream. I no longer wish to harm anyone or seek vengeance. My mother was my hero, someone who managed everything in her life with a smile on her face. Though her image has been reduced to a mere tiny human in my memory, I still miss her. She is a part of my life that I can never let go. Leaving her was the hardest thing that I had ever done in my life. I was at conflict with her, but I knew that her biggest dream in life was to see mine get fulfilled. There was no way I could get my dream of being successful, as long as I stayed by her side, pretending to live the lie she had created. Maybe she keeps messaging me because she understands that my dream is her dream too.

With an ever-growing dissatisfaction in all cells of my body, I knew something had to change. At school or at home, I had evolved into a version of myself I really did not like, mainly because I was trying to 'fit in' and be like everyone else in my social circles. It culminated in confusion about my identity, as well as unhappiness and bitterness on a personal level. Seeking happiness and pursuing our dreams has a price and for me, that cost me my family and friendship.

It was when I was trying to fit with the new social circle that one day, I received a message from my mom saying that grandfather had passed away. I dealt with this guilt for long because I didn't know how to go back, how to say that I was sorry, and I just didn't know what to do. So many years had passed, and I hadn't been in contact with anyone, so I tried to go but didn't know how to face the truth. My feelings had overpowered me. Perhaps, all I needed to know, at that time, was a moment of awareness, where I could address my feelings as they were, but I let them control me. As remorseful as it was, it had fueled me with the fire to do what my grandfather always wanted me to do. I never listened to him before, but his words would echo in my ears and maybe I could offer peace to his soul. Reflecting on my last days at home, I do feel bad for staying away from everyone, I even left without telling anyone or saying good bye, so how could I go back or what would I say to them?

Guilt made me stand with Ugowens and it proved to be challenging for my personal growth. They prevent you from living in love, creating in love, and enjoying yourself in love. It made me see the past as something that could have been better or things I could have done differently. This wish itself is the biggest obstruction in life, for this is the biggest lie that anyone could live. I was living this lie of remorse which prevented happiness in my life. What my mother did was not a lie, it was a secret to help me live a better life beside a man who took care of us. I had never looked at life this way, but analyzing my feelings helped me to get out of their control. It created a moment of awareness within me.

Our experiences are designed to inform, support, and benefit us, not cause us to contract into fear and remorse. No one can cause me emotional pain, unless I let the pain ignite within me. My actions are my responsibility, and if they come from fear rather than love, they will create painful consequences.

Each time I choose not to act on frightened parts of my personality, I create more energy. The frightened parts of my personality come less frequently and with less intensity, and the loving parts fill more and more of my consciousness. Eventually, the frightened parts of my personality will lose their power over me entirely, and only the loving parts will remain. When this happens, guilt, fear, or regret will become opportunities that lead to exactly where I want to go, to fulfillment and awareness.

I have stopped avoiding my feelings now, I confront them when I face them. Understanding them gives me the courage to control my response towards them. I still feel scared or remorse at times, but I am no longer hesitant in analyzing them. When I courageously face the thing I fear, I automatically experience the growth I have been seeking. Fear is a product of my mind and since it's a mental process, I can use my mind to stop it and live a more satisfying life.

When we back away from a fear-inducing situation or person, our fear grows larger and larger until we deal with it. It can get to the point that it dominates our thinking and feeling during the day, and often keeps us awake at night.

However, if we face the fear, it will leave us. Our ability to confront and act properly despite our fears, is the key to our mental freedom. It makes us happier and allows us to become more successful. Although it's never easy to face and walk through fear, when we understand what's really causing our anxiety, we will know how to reverse it.

When we go through life reacting to what's going on in the outside world, it's easy to let doubt and worry take over our thoughts and emotions. I want to help myself eliminate fear and create the life of love. I willingly release the thoughts and things that clutter my mind.

Without love, every experience of anger, jealousy, resentment, and fear sends us spinning out of control. Ugowens have always made me realize that I am always right and someone else is wrong, I am a victim and someone else is a villain.

Love brings our awareness to others and ourselves. Love opens our mind and heart to others and ourselves. When we choose to become sensitive and caring instead of frightened and selfish, our anger turns to appreciation, our jealousy to gratitude, and our resentment to caring. We cannot lose our orientation: when our deeds harm others, we are in fear, and when we create harmony, sharing, and reverence for life, we deal with love. The ground beneath us is always solid. Gravity pulls us towards earth and love pulls towards life.

I sat quietly on the side bench, watching the people execute an array of energy, and wondering about life. I let my eyes wander the whole space around me and so much time had passed watching people and thinking about how our lives worked. The sun was setting, and the air was getting cooler, I removed a glove and let my fingers fall to the surface of the bench, the heat of the day had escaped its surface, inviting the cold energy of the night. It sure is a way of accepting the nature for what it offers.

A man was coming slowly from the right side. His charming looks did make people turn their heads to watch him. He had tousled, dark-brown hair, which was thick and lustrous. His eyes were mesmerizing with deep feelings. His face was strong and defined, his features molded from granite. He had dark eyebrows, which sloped downwards in a serious expression. His usual smile had drawn into a hard line across his face.

I just realized that I had been dreaming with my eyes open while staring at him.

He came closer and sat by me. He sat calmly, feeling the air around him. I watched him taking deep breaths.

"I remember sitting on the other side of this bench the last time we were here," Emre said without looking at me,

"I didn't know you would come to sit here again. The view from here is amazing, isn't it, Meryl?"

"How do you know it's me?" I asked in wonder.

"I can feel people around me better than you can see them," Emre said with a grin, "I come here every evening, it reminds me of the last time I visited France. I didn't know many places, so I found my peace here."

"I did not want to react the way I did to your request," I said slowly.

"It's always okay to react, as long as you remember to say sorry later, something my mother used to say," Emre chuckled, "A fine lady, who raised two boys and a girl."

"I remember her sentence because she said that to me every time I had a fight with my brother. We were playing in the park, like this one, and he told me not to take the longest ride and I didn't listen to him. So, when I fell and injured my knee and my parents asked him why he had let me go on the big rides. He told them that I didn't listen to him. They told me that it was very important to listen to my brother. I got angry because instead of looking at my pain, they would rather focus on making me listen to the perfect son they have," Emre started talking about his personal life for the first time and I had no idea why he was opening up.

"My parents were really fond of my older brother; I was the youngest of my siblings. They had always told me to be obedient to the older one, for he was the wisest of us all. But I hated that since I could remember, I wanted my own self to be the one who would be in charge. Or at least, the favored one. Maybe that was not the case but that's how I always felt because we were supposed to listen to our eldest brother," Emre continued, looking straight, "As I grew older, I never liked listening to him, but I had to do it out of the fear that my mom would make me apologize to him. I didn't want him to be the boss, but he was always telling me to do what was right. I remember the day he was leaving to join the military school, he came to say good bye to my room and saw me smoking. He told me that it was a bad habit and I was too young to do all this.

'What are you going to do? Tell Mom and Dad? You might save your perfect son's seat before leaving me in peace. Go ahead, take your shining medal that has been yours since I was a kid.'"

"I was angry at him for being my boss all the time."

"'I did all that to protect you from harm because Mom and Dad would make me promise them, to look after you but I didn't know you felt that way.'

'Yeah, well, you did a good job at earning yourself the medal of a better son all those times. Go ahead, tell them and they will let me know what a good example you were for me. I thought I could be at peace once you move away.'

'I will not tell upon you and I have no intention of making your life miserable. I just looked after you out of love.'"

"My brother left me without saying goodbye and I thought I had done good by fighting with him, for at least he didn't tell about my wrong habits to my parents. While I wasn't doing well in my university, my brother wanted to marry a girl from another religion. My parents did not approve of it, so they had told him a no. My brother came to convince my parents on the weekend, but they refused to listen to him on that topic. Seeing him in a uniform reminded me of our childhood days, when we pretended to be soldiers saluting each other."

"I didn't talk much at the dinner where he was trying to convince my parents, but it was a clear no from them. I had never seen them say no to him like that. Maybe we were all cold and he was the only one with a compassion for us all. He told me before leaving, that he would be glad if I understood his love for that girl, but I didn't."

"After he left us again, I was a bit relieved that the perfect son was not so perfect anymore, though I didn't say it out loud. My sister was the only one talking to him and the last time he called home, he asked me to keep in touch with him. He hated not being able to talk to Mom and Dad like before. Even though I had told him that I didn't care about him, he would still send me messages on my birthday and other occasions."

"Almost a year had passed, and I didn't reply to him for anything."

"On New Year's Eve, we were all sitting together because my parents made sure that the family would get together for dinner once my brother arrived. Even though my parents did not agree with my brother, they still waited for him with the utmost anxiety. Mom had cooked his favorite duck and I still remember that doorbell sound when my father ran to open the door and I thought to myself that once again, it's all about him."

"My mom came smiling from the kitchen and my sister also ran to meet her favorite brother. I leaned my head back to see the man in shining medals make his glorious entry. But I saw two officers at the door who lowered their caps and told my dad the sad news, 'I have been asked to inform you that your son has been reported dead in…'"

Tears fell from Emre's eyes on his hands that were resting in his lap. I was so sad and still wondering why he was telling me this.

The laughter of the children in the park had died along with the light of the day. The park grew even darker. Soon the shadows of the trees would blend into the blackness and their silhouettes against the sky will grow less pronounced.

"'…on the behalf of the Secretary of Defense, I extend to you and your family my deepest sympathy in your great loss.'

I can still recall those words," Emre wiped his tears, "My mom fell to the ground and my sister ran to help her, while my dad stood still in the door, staring in the air, and saying nothing. I pulled myself to stand up but couldn't gather the courage to move beyond that spot. The sadness drained through me rather than skating over my skin. It travelled through every cell of mine to sabotage the liveliness within me. I stood there, as I felt my heart cracking like glass, spreading its pieces throughout my body. I could hardly bare the sight of the depression that had overtaken our lives. Tears streaming down cheeks, falling to the ground like raindrops."

Emre took a deep breath, "I stood there, longing to see my brother, even if it was to fight with him. I just wished he had come, just to scold me, or tell upon me, or steal all the love from my parents. I just wish he had come to take my place altogether and be the perfect son forever. My heart slowed, as I realized the coldness that had dawned upon us and LOVE, just like that, had left us, for we had taken it for granted for a long time."

"You know, Meryl, disgust is a very strong emotion with negativity, but it can have a very powerful impact on you. That day, I was disgusted at many of the feelings that I had harbored since childhood. Feeling disgusted with those made me realize that I needed to address my problems that were making me suffer every day."

"The sorrow grew more profound with every passing day. My sister later told me that our brother had volunteered to fight at the border after we became cold towards him."

"After I joined the university to learn about politics, I still couldn't get over my sorrow. My feelings were dominated by it and every memory of my brother made me realize that all he ever did was out of love and all that I ever did was out of fear. The worst part, was that fear had stayed and love suffered the loss of leaving this place. Maybe love gave up or sacrificed itself, for fear had overpowered the house of the people that were dear to love. I can say this all now but at that time, I didn't know what I was doing. My feelings of being cold towards my brother before he left, were killing me. So, I left my home after finishing my studies."

"I told my parents that I got a job in the Middle East, but I left to take refuge somewhere else. I really don't think they cared, for we hardly talked to each other after the death of my brother. My mom kept herself busy and my dad nodded to everything we said about our lives. He was not himself and my mom always jumped to the doorbell, thinking that someday her elder son would appear there. I believed that they wouldn't care where I went, as long as someone didn't come to them with the news of my death."

"My mom sat silently and bid me a kiss without saying much. I went to my dad and he looked busy without anything to do than just stare outside the window. I sat near him, held his hand, and told him that I was leaving. He didn't say anything but when I was about to get up, he placed his other hand over mine and said, 'Children are like birds that we hate to set free, but the higher they soar, the more joyous we are,' he stood up with tears in his eyes, 'Make sure you don't fly as high as your brother.' He hugged me and I felt worse with depression. I had never seen him cry before. Maybe it was good, but I needed to leave, for I kept blaming myself every time I saw their sad faces."

Emre turned his face towards mine, "You keep asking me how I manage to work through my feelings without my sight and I told you I do it through my feelings. The reason is that I got a training in being more consciously aware of my senses."

"After seeing despair in my house, I did suffer from guilt for a long time. I was feeling that my eyes were getting weak. So, I went to my optician again and again with the same complaint that his prescribed glasses made me feel dizzy after some time. He told me that my depression was causing me to lose sight. I tried to work on it but living with guilt and depression was not helping."

"There was a clear evidence of a psychosomatic component to vision loss, as stress is an important cause, not just a consequence, of progressive vision loss."

"Vision loss is considered to be irreversible and often progressive, my doctor told me. Patients experience continuous mental stress due to worries, anxiety, or fear with secondary consequences such as depression and social isolation. While prolonged mental stress is clearly a cause of vision loss, it was aggravating the situation for me. My sight loss was progressive, and my doctor was worried. He told me that a few years back, one of his patients went to the eastern mountains to heal a vision loss that was similar to mine."

"He didn't know if the patient was healed but he said that he did write to him afterwards, saying that he was doing better in life. 'If any of my patients ever experienced a progressive vision loss, I tell them about the place in the Himalayan region where people with disabilities go to heal themselves.' He gave me his e-mail which had the address and the way to contact that place. I didn't tell anyone at home about my situation and left the house, telling everyone that I got a job in the Middle East."

"I followed the address that took me to the northern areas of Pakistan. I met two people there who questioned me about the reasons for my visit. I left all my electronics, metal devices, and my cell phone at their place. They were two brothers who lived in a small house at the base of the mountains and worked for the specialist that lived in the mountains. I left with them with only a bag of few clothes and shoes."

"After travelling for a whole day, we arrived at a valley that was like heaven on earth, I had never seen any place as beautiful as that. It was fascinating, there was a whole new world there. I was surprised to see so much life there. I thought it would just be a few people working, with an expert living in a cave, away from the society, and would heal me with the help of some leaves and green potions. But to my surprise, it was a world with all the beauty and life, without the disturbance of mobiles and laptops. People lived in small houses surrounded by trees, and spent their days working in gardens and eating the fruits of nature.

"The men told me that they didn't even need money to live there, they managed to keep their community healthy and alive by making each family responsible for their gardens and maintenance of their houses. They had a small community and the head of the community was an old man, who was the therapist that I was going to see. I became more hopeful and to my surprise, it was a man a lot younger than what I had imagined. He told me that he was seventy years old, but it was hard to believe him."

"'People here don't age like the people from your world, I understand why you would think that,' he told me, 'I am Kabir and this is the community that I created to save our families. We fled from the war during the Indo-Pak partition and took refuge in these valleys. We were seven kids then and we were separated from our parents during migration. Me and my six cousins helped each other climb the mountain for days and fled from the horror that occupied the rest of the world. Our parents had told us to stick together for our safety, and so we did. We never knew what happened to our parents, but we managed to survive after coming here. There was a small garden here, we would play like kids with small stick-houses and then as we grew up, we made those into real houses. Now, we make sure we live like we did when we were small kids, and try to keep a community that dwells on nature without money or disputes. It does get challenging at times, but I try to heal the poison of greed out of our community with awareness. This is how we have preserved our pure lives, but some wonderers did come here and spread the story of the uncontaminated life. Since then, people do come here to heal themselves and we try to help. So, tell me, what brings a strong young man like you here?'"

"I told him about my vision loss with every passing day. I told him that it happened after my brother died and I missed him."

"'You don't only miss him; you are sad that he left you and you couldn't do anything about it. You blame yourself for something else too,' he told me. 'The progressive vision loss cannot be reversed, but I can help you seek awareness through other senses, as long as you have your sight. It will help you get rid of the load of depression and guilt that you carry with you." I agreed and followed his instructions from that day onward."

"With every sunrise, he would bring me to the riverside and teach me to become more self-aware by mastering my feelings. I spent hours mastering my feelings with his mindful techniques and became more conscious."

"Self-awareness gave me a deep understanding of my emotions, strengths, weaknesses, and drives. I learnt that people with strong self-awareness are neither overtly critical, nor unrealistically hopeful. Rather, they are honest with themselves and with others. The keystone of self-awareness is recognizing a feeling as it happens. If we don't understand our feelings from moment to moment, we are unlikely to achieve the level of insight and self-understanding required for peace."

"He would imply that there was evidence that disease sometimes begins in the form of negative thought impulse. Such an impulse may be passed from one mind to another, by suggestion, or created by an individual in his own mind. I had caused my vision to be impaired by inculcating extreme feelings of depression and pain. Depression is nothing more than suppressed anxiety caused by a fearful subconscious mind. Depression is the symptom, but until we treat the primary cause, there is never going to be permanent change. The cause of depression is having a conscious mind being filled with worry and doubt through the five senses."

"The opposite of depression is acceleration, which is simply an expression of well-being caused by having a faithful subconscious mind, brought on by bringing understanding and knowledge in the conscious mind."

"The more I experienced and explored my own feelings, the more I realized how necessary these feelings were. It's good for us to spend time exploring the unknowns. It gives us an opportunity to discover who we really are and what life is all about."

"The only remedy to fear is love. The only place where I can inculcate love beyond fear, is in myself."

"To create with love required that I needed to identify fear in myself and challenge it by not acting on it and instead, act from the most loving part of my personality. The frightened parts of my personality were those that I experienced as anger, jealousy, resentment, terror, depression, and humiliation. The loving parts of my personality were those that I experienced as gratitude, appreciation, caring, and patience. The most important thing that he taught me was about the senses other than my five physical senses."

"From a five-sensory perspective, it may appear impossible to be grateful or appreciative of an occurrence that I did not want to happen. From a multi-sensory perspective, it is an opportunity to grow spiritually, and opportunities to grow spiritually are always being offered to us in the intimacy of our own experiences, no matter what is happening outside of us."

"It was the time to come to terms with challenging the energy of fear within me, to use my courage to experience fear fully, emotionally, in terms of physical sensations in my body, and to encounter it by choosing consciously to act with an intention of love. With every passing moment of practicing awareness, I became more conscious of my feelings. I gradually lost my sight but saw things more clearly. I could feel the world better than I had ever seen it. And here I am, sensing everything around me better than ever."

"Love, you will learn, is unconditional, and you cannot put conditions if you want to be in a state of pure love. The problems in our personal lives result from a desire to change those that we love or feel for. It is okay to love people and decide to stay away from them. We don't have to hate people in order to disagree with them. You can choose to live apart in disagreement and still care for one another. This is life. Once you realize that you have different ways of living, you choose your own path, but you don't have to hate your associations as an excuse to be apart. They are still a part of your memories and you can miss them too, while choosing to live a different lifestyle. Pure love teaches us a lot of ways to let love be the driving source of our decisions, not fear or hate."

Emre's story was challenging and made me realize the power of our own strengths.

Chapter 15

I have lived my entire life focusing on the circumstances that have been driven by my feelings. I now find ways to drive my own world by addressing these feelings. I stand here in the darkness once again, seeking the power within my subconscious mind. It is dark and cold, but there is a path on the far end, which seems brighter than the place I am standing on. As I walk on, I feel someone approaching me from behind.

"You are the one whose dad abandoned her," I heard a voice.

"You knew she would be alone, but you still left her to live your own life," came another voice.

It is annoying to hear all this, but it was true, this is what I was before. I was living with these doubts and sorrows.

"The only person you ever trusted; made you live the biggest lie of your life."

"You hate your life. You hate everyone."

I feel a cold chill shoot all the way up my spine. I am nervous. I walk faster and can feel how badly my legs are shaking. I have the chills, but I am going on. There are countless butterflies in my stomach just floating around, causing tension deep inside of my body. I feel queasy and look around in search for help. But the only things I can see are some forms coming from the shadow behind me.

"Please help me," I manage to say out loud to I don't know whom, but my eyes are focused on the path of light. I feel the shadows closing in, so I gain more pace and pull the strength to walk faster than ever. I think that I am running, but my legs seem frailer.

"You made a promise to your grandfather and now you are stuck in a turmoil." The shadow touches my shoulders and I can feel the pain; I quickly start running and leave it behind.

My muscles are getting sore and tight. It would hurt if anyone would touch me.

"What if you never win this and realize that there really is no way of winning over your feelings?"

I keep running and hear a voice calling my name, from far in the distant light. I am running towards the light; I can feel the grassy solid ground now, instead of the hard-cold floor. I don't hear the voices anymore. The sky above me is changing color to a crimson white. There are no people to cheer me, yet I feel lighter. I am in a happy, peaceful, and tranquil place, slowly letting out all the nervousness and pressure that was building up inside of me. I am ready to run my heart out and kick in with a forceful push.

I know I am better at leaving fear behind and sprint on towards the brighter light. My path has already gained light, I gladly look back but see a figure that is horrible enough to tear my whole life apart. It's not ugly, yet its presence is frightfully overpowering. His horrifying stature is magnificently commanding, and if I didn't know it better, it fitted the definition of Fear, that Amour had described for me. I almost trip over and feel dizzy with fright.

I manage to look away and run as fast as my legs can carry me. His glimpse was enough to shoot my confidence to naught. I want to take one giant leap and reach the bright path, but my feet are heavy with fright. I don't want to look at Fear anymore. I want to win life over Fear. I can see the sky getting brighter with the bright path approaching nearer. My heart is pounding rapidly, my body is extremely hot, worn out, and exhausted.

Reaching the bright side is the only thing on my mind. I block out from the race by the thought of Fear, but quickly put my focus to my goal. I am running at full speed; I am about to reach it soon. My goal is my sole focus, now as I smile. Fear seems to have vanished from my side and I push myself forward. I feel the sun shining bright on my face and I know that I have reached the brighter side.

At this moment, I know I have defeated Fear, when I see Amour. I start to cry, tears of joy and completeness run down my face. I feel worn out, but I don't care for I have beaten my fears. I still have the chills from excitement.

I realize that the only thing that we get out of life is what we put into it. I have now learned this through experience. We must inculcate the courage to explore our feelings and achieve our goals. Once we start exploring, then we open the door towards much success and happiness in the future. The race in life is as much psychological as it is physiological. Personal abilities determine our achievements, but our perception of these abilities is the defining factor in how we live our lives.

I feel like I am running every day in my life, angry at someone, regretting something, or hoping for things to change from the outside.

I paused when I come near Amour, I feel like a few days back, I would have quit, but my dedication seems undoubted now. Amour smiles at me as I regain my positivity in his presence, but doesn't ask me to stop. He points to the mountain ahead of me. I see a shadow near a tree, standing next to a horse. It is a beautiful sight, with the sun shining its radiance on the lady, and her dress flowing with the wind, like the horse's mane. I have not reached my goal yet. I have conquered fear for now and I need to reach to the top of the mountain to that horse to gain more consciousness. I start up the small, steep, inclining mountain.

I see a man reaching out to pull me up. I take his hand, but the ground is slippery. I cannot figure out who it is, for his bright yellow hair reflect the sun in my eyes. He is wearing a yellow robe and marching on, while holding my hand. It's hard for my feet to maintain a solid grip against the surface. My shins and thighs are starting to burn. This sensation is getting worse and I think I will slip away. I grasp his hand tighter and it gets harder to climb up.

I want to reach the top to my destination. "It's OK if you don't make it to the top, I am at the perfect place," I hear the man whisper; the sun is blinding me, and I cannot figure out the path. I try hard to just cross the slippery side. I keep pushing even as the pain gets worse. I hold his hands with both of mine and try to help myself up. I can do it, I tell myself. "Of course, you can. You have me as your help," he whispers again, but I still couldn't see him clearly.

I push myself to go a little further, holding on to him. My mind starts to drift away. I think of all the moments when I believed I was right and left everything and everyone without saying anything. I recall all those times when I wouldn't even reply to anyone's messages because I think life is about me only.

The sun is beating down on my back as my feet claw at the slippery slope. With every step I take, my toes sink into the slippery rocks and my lungs grasp for air. Everything feels the way it should, as I plunge towards my destination. I clutch his hands with my sweaty palms, promising myself not to let go.

As the man helps me up, my feet slip again. I am struggling hard to pull myself, but this man's presence brings back all the selfish memories that make it hard for me to concentrate. I finally let go of his hand and pull the strength to walk up without him. All at once, my foot ceases to travel onwards and the woman with the horse starts to blur like a scanty image.

The colors spin and merge as I still struggle to pull myself up. I am not able to speak, the feeling of losing my goal causes me to splash my arms randomly around me. I am falling and falling down. The probable thump of the ground doesn't come and instead, I'm still falling and now it is completely black. Not every race in life is a victory, no matter how much we think we have conquered, there still are certain things left that hold us back.

These races are either failures that will cause us to doubt ourselves, or stepping stones on our path to our goals like valuable lessons. We can always move past our perceived failures, take away something of value, and keep working towards our goals.

Life never brings failures, just the value of feelings and experiences that show us the mental demons which we must learn to overcome. It is how we move forward that counts. Part of moving forward in life is analyzing why we live.

Not every race is the same. Every day brings new circumstances. We cannot let our feelings for external pressures decide how we want to deal with life. We cannot let fear and doubts limit our experiences. In fact, we can utilize the ugowens to bring out the best in us.

Chapter 16

I did not feel upset but a little down after my experience through my subconscious. I had clearly underestimated the power of ugowens. I wanted to feel better. I did not know what I was going to do in the next challenge or will the next challenge in the book be the same one. I was having some mixed emotions and I knew whose presence could rectify this negativity. So, I went out to the park and waited for him to arrive in the evening. I told him that I wanted to take the trip to Canada. I was not certain if I was going to meet my mom for sure, but I decided to go and clear my mind.

Canada is a beautiful country with natural attractions. It reminds me of my childhood and early years. It's my homeland and stays in my heart no matter where I am. We had a three-night stay at a great hotel in Toronto. One King West Hotel was on the path system so we could go out with light jackets and explore without going out in the winds. The room I had was really big, equipped with a mini kitchen. I had a queen bed and another nice armchair. I felt comfortable at nights. I didn't think that three nights were enough to enjoy a place like this, but as soon as I got up the next day, I wanted to go home and meet my mom. Maybe it was the feeling of coming to my own country. I had run away from here, but I didn't want to run away anymore. I wanted to be here and visit my home.

Emre had conferences during the days. He told me I could join him if I felt like it, but I told him that I wanted to go home or at least, try to meet my mom, so that I would always remember that I tried.

Mississauga is about 40 minutes outside of downtown Toronto, accessible by the Gardiner Expressway East-West, or by the 427 North onto the 401 East-West. Most parts of Mississauga are peaceful. 70% of the living population are core families.

As I pass the houses, I recall that my mom loved staying here, whenever she would talk about this place she would say, "I can never leave this place, and neither should you, Meryl, but if you ever decide to, then always remember that this is where I will always live. Living in Mississauga to me means that I'm living a social and a happy life because I like to socialize with strangers, and I'm always happy because of what I'm able to do on a daily basis."

Mississauga is a slightly more affluent ethnic suburb, full of mostly Asian people. Parts of it are sort of ghetto, there's a big mall called Square One there, and sort of a downtown Mississauga area with some bars and clubs. Mississauga is a mix of industrial parks, high rises, strip malls, and shopping centers, interspersed with a lot of nice, residential neighborhoods.

I was visiting my old house after seven years and still the vicinity seemed untouched by the usual hustle and bustle of the huge, polluted, metropolitan cities. I just had to close my eyes and every moment of my childhood flashed before my eyes. I felt like I had never gone away, and everything felt as similar as yesterday. There were steep stone-steps leading towards the house, obstructed by a small gate made of flaking rusty iron.

There were a few residents strolling along the stoned street. There were groups of small children playing in the park close to our house. I remembered myself swinging on those once. Their mothers stood beside, chattering loudly as if no one was listening.

After walking a few more steps, I felt my feet getting heavier. All the reasons that I didn't need to do this came flooding back to my head. I could not let these thoughts overpower me and gathered the strength to go ahead. I was close to the door. Before turning the knob, I let my fingers walk over the door of the house that I had grown up in. Even in the warm spring sunshine, there was a coolness to it. I closed my eyes to absorb the tears that might run down.

I turned the knob and found it open. My heart almost skipped a beat, I left the door knob and stepped back, through the door I saw her laying down the table. With butterflies in my stomach and head buzzing with nervousness, there was no way that I could face her. I saw her and couldn't go away. I had to meet my mom. The nervous sensation was taken over by my love for her.

My mother was one for fun and happiness. It was so fun, all those everyday adventures. I could still feel her excitement at seeing a simple flower or the way the light played upon the path. In a life so ordinary, it was her that was extraordinary, not because she was given so much, but because she made it that way. As the baker turns flour and water to bread, as God turns seed and water to flower, Mother turned the mundane into fascination and love; she was my heaven, my superhero.

My mom's apron was a primary of my childhood, patterned with all things western, from teapots to the plates. When I thought of it, the aromas of her fresh-baking came flooding in to my brain, my heart jumped, and there was that moment of tranquility. I had seen her in that apron most of my day, smiling and asking me to join her for something delicious she had made just for me. She would have this amazing smile that was enough to wipe away your worries and all the negative things would vanish, once I would start eating those. I approached her and she was laying down the table with the same apron, but there was no smile on her face. She was lost in her thought and did not realize my presence.

"Mom," I said, as cold shivered my entire body.

I saw her in that apron once again, but not a smile, rather a surprise and her hands that held the plate started shivering. She saw me and tried to hold back her tears. I had never seen her cry, but she stood still looking at me.

"Meeryyll," her voice was trembling, and I still didn't see a smile, but a woman standing in a shock. She looked older now, maybe it was my absence that had made her age quicker than how she was supposed to. "You are here," she came closer to touch me.

"I hope it's not a dream. Tell me," she looked at me with tearful eyes, "Tell me it's not a dream. Please tell me you are here."

"It's not, Mom," I had to say that, she was patting my face with trembling hands, "I am home."

I held her hands and brought her to sit at the table. "You can relax," I told her.

"Look here," she pointed to the kitchen with tearful eyes, "I made your favorite chicken." She got up to get it. She was not herself, she was shaking and talking despite me telling her to stop. She was so excited, "Look here, I knew you would come one day but you never replied to me so I didn't know when, but I knew you would come. I have been making your favorite dish every day for the past so many years. My friends who come to visit me say that I am crazy and if children grow up, we need to give them space, but I always say, what space? My baby is my sunshine, she knows I cannot live without her. She left by mistake and she will return," my mother just continued in excitement and wouldn't stop. "So, see now, who is right. Me, of course. I knew you would come. You are my love and I am your peace; I knew you would miss me and will come to see me. I told everyone that my Meryl is a gem and she will come back to me, if not in my lifetime, then surely when I die, but I knew you would come. I am glad you chose to come during my lifetime. I would hate not hugging you if you came to my grave."

My mom cut a slice from the chicken, "Look, your favorite. Tell me how it is. I hope you like it." She was smiling, wiping her tears again and again.

"Mom, please sit down," I tried to settle her down, "I can't believe you would make this every day, Mom. I am sorry for not replying to your messages or calls."

"Oh no, dear, if the price is seeing you after seven years, I would do it every day for the next seven years. It was nothing, all for you, the sunshine of my winters."

Her hands were still trembling, but she told me to eat, I couldn't swallow, so I assured her that I would eat later.

I apologized to her again, but she comforted me, "I never need your apology, Meryl, I give you wings so you can fly, but hope that you always feel thirsty to return to drink water from my home. You know, as parents, we cherish your flights, but a small part of us betrays us to wish that you would always return to us. Even if it's for a little while, we want to be felt needed by you." She hugs me and presses me close to her. Before I could let go of the hug like I used to when I was little, I melt into her love. Her hands are folded around my back, drawing me in closer. I can feel my body shake, crying for the missed time we could never make back, crying to release the tension of those seven long years. Running her hands through my hair, she kissed my forehead and kept me close to her. "Do not leave like this ever again. Please, don't leave like that," she whispered to me.

The warmth of her body met my cold skin. One of her hands clasped around my lower back, the other stroked my hair. With each soft touch, more tears fell, tears neither of us wiped away. After so many years, I had the chance to mend my mistakes. I spent the whole day with her. She told me about who had left from the neighborhood and how many new friends she had made. I loved listening to her after all those years. I went to rest in my room, which was exactly how I had left it.

"Of course, you didn't think I would let anyone touch anything." She told me to rest while she made dinner, "Oh, and Samantha will come to join me for the dinner with her father. You remember Mr. Remy, right? We usually get together for dinner. We still talk about you so much."

My mom left me to relax there for a while, I couldn't take a nap, so I sat down to look over the things that I had always cherished as a little girl. I opened my album box and so many memories came rushing back to me. I could never understand what it was about our memories that made us hold on to them. To preserve them and be remembered that way, from time to time. Maybe we cherish memories because memories allow us to relive the most beautiful parts of our lives, anytime we want. Process of remembering involves a diverse set of cognitive neural processes that is a copy of original experience. We experience pleasure every time we remember our cherished memory.

Knowledge is all just plain old memories straight up. All my life that I could recall, is based on those memories. Everyone that I loved, I cherished them because of my memories of those people. The things that are not in front of me exist for me in the form of memories. We cherish memories, because we are mentally and socially, in terms of our identity, almost completely composed of memories. The identity then becomes a strong part of our subconscious and if the subconscious did not use them as identity, then surely there would be nothing to cherish or live up to.

I shared so many of my pictures with Samantha. I realized that my personality was a derivative of the sum of those memories. I would feel hollow inside if it were not for them. Maybe that's why my mind never wanted to let go of those moments and found an excuse to visit them from time to time. I could cherish those feelings, but if I let them take power over me every time I recalled them, then surely, I would be inviting the negative in my life.

Memories were just recollections; I could filter my mind to recall those that brought pleasure and learn from those that once brought misery to me. It meant my subconscious was in my control and my feelings served me, rather than having me serve them.

After a few hours, I went down to meet my mom. She was preparing the dinner. She saw me and started talking with excitement again.

"You know, I told them that you are here," she went on, "They are so happy and can't wait to meet you." She brushed aside her hair and I saw a scar on her neck that I did not recall from before. "Honey, you remember Samantha; I mean, what am I asking, of course you do. You both were inseparable since your childhood." My mother looked at me to say something, but I didn't, so she continued after a pause, "You know, sometimes, I think maybe you both had a fight, so you decided to go away from her too, but I could never understand why, because Samantha came for many days to ask about you."

"I never had a fight with her, but I want to ask you something, Mom, that I never had the guts to ask before," I pulled the courage to muster that out of my mouth. I knew grandfather had told me not to say that to her, but I thought it was necessary to express the truth, so I was going to tell her that I knew about the lie and left because of that.

"Of course, my dear, anything, I am all ears," she sat by my side.

I took a deep breath, "I think I will take a walk," I got up to breathe some fresh air.

"I will be waiting for you right here. Don't go far and remember to be back before the dinner, my dear," my mother smiled at me.

I left to stand outside for a while in the fresh air. I needed to breathe, I think I did feel better after seeing my mom and letting out so many emotions. It was so good to be myself and I literally felt at home. I slowly strolled to the park across the road, I would come here every day and play as long as I liked. It was the most beautiful park for me.

The park was nothing like those of the smaller towns. Theirs were little formal gardens for the settled that had retired there for the quiet life. They had benches, ornamental trees, flowers year-round, and a small water fountain. There was a vendor with hotdogs and burgers, my mom wouldn't let me have more than one.

My mother would tell me sometimes that when her hair would turn grey like grandpa's, she would sit on these benches to spend her evenings, watching the sunset. Her hair had turned grey now, but she seemed to have forgotten that. I stood close to one of the swings that was my favorite. Sometimes, Samantha would save it for me and when I would return after a bathroom break, I would see her fighting with the other kids for not letting them sit on it. I smiled back at all those memories.

"I knew you would come here," I heard a familiar voice come closer to me from behind.

I quickly turned to see that it was whom I had expected. I wanted to hug her like old times, but so many years stood like cold ice between us. I looked at her and tried to say something, but words seemed to be stuck in my throat.

"When Aunt Afua called to tell me that you were back, I couldn't believe it till I saw you standing here." Samantha came close to me, "So, why are you really here?"

"I wanted to meet Mom."

"Why now, when you just vanished and all we saw was a crying mother for years?"

"I feel terrible, but I had my reasons and I don't justify them anymore. But I want to be with her now."

"What about me? You can't just come here and expect us all to be fine."

"I am sorry, Samantha. I didn't know how to act, I found out something and I needed to be away."

"Sorry? That's all you have to say for the way you left? And found out what, that my dad is your dad too?"

I felt horror run through my veins, "You knew that?"

"Yes, I did. I heard Dad talk to my mom about it. They were fighting about it. So what, Meryl? I learned, but I never ran away like you did. I heard them and I was upset at first, but my dad made that decision when Mom had left him. He explained it to my mom when I heard them fighting about it. But later, I realized that Dad took care of both of us. I was disappointed at first, but I never had to suffer for any of that. In fact, I got to have a sister in the form of a friend. But you left like a coward and you had no idea what your mom went through," she yelled at me.

"When I found out, I went home to Grandpa, he didn't deny it but made me promise to never tell my mom because she never wanted me to know. I couldn't live like that, it was killing me."

"I never told my dad too, but you know he was already going through a hard time, my mom was fighting with him for looking after your mom when you were away. He took her to hospitals and spent nights looking after her."

"I feel bad okay, so I came back," I was crying.

"Came back now so you can leave again when you feel like. And that woman, who was more supportive to me than my own mother, would suffer again. I went to my dad and told him that I would help him too." Samantha looked around because her voice had gotten louder, she came closer and said softly, "Your mother got an infection and then developed a tumor in her throat, we looked after her all those times, when all that would have made her feel better was a phone call from you. Just a reminder that her daughter valued her," Samantha stepped away and sat on the bench.

I was crying and listening quietly, I didn't know what to do. I felt worse but I didn't come to cause distress or pain. I had come to heal myself, but I was selfish and thinking about myself again. I should have come to heal the pain of those I had been hurting for a long time.

"I know me saying sorry is not enough," I sat down next to Samantha, "I am not asking you to forgive me either, but I want you to know that I didn't know how to handle my feelings before, and I wish you can find it some day in your heart to forgive me."

"She might say that she forgave you, but you were not here, and I saw the pain you gave her when she would come from painful therapies, yet she would check her phone to see if you would talk to her. You talk about your feelings, but no one ever did anything to hurt you. It was always like that, Meryl, everyone trying to cheer you, everyone trying to make you comfortable, yet you never did anything to cheer us. In fact, you again thought of the ways in which the world had harmed you. It was all about you. I was here with them but all they talked about was you. That poor lady never stopped, she still makes your favorite meal every day, saying that you will be here one day. Then, we stopped talking about you, and I saw my parents were moving on and I would visit your mom sometimes to check on her. We were just going to join her for dinner but here you are now, the magnificent Meryl, who appears to surprise us so we can give her a merry welcome." Samantha was angrier than ever.

We stayed quiet after her yelling had stopped. We sat there for a long time. It was getting dark.

"You say that you are sorry, but I wonder that if you are here because you are sorry or just finding an excuse to let out your emotions for your own therapy or whatever you have planned to do."

"I really am sorry."

"See you at dinner." Samantha left me there alone, I cried my heart out. The tears burst forth like water from a dam, spilling down my face. I felt the muscles of my chin tremble like a small child and I looked towards my house, as if its image could soothe me. It took something out of me I didn't know I had left to give. I cleared my face and sent out a sigh of relief. I walked towards my house; every step made me feel lighter. Sometimes, the very remedy we seek in life is always out of reach, as are we.

I freshened up, wearing an old dress that my mom had once bought for my first day at work. It was still hanging there untouched. I came down and Samantha had already arrived with her dad. Mr. Remy greeted me, and Samantha and I exchanged low welcomes.

The dinner started very quietly with the sounds of our spoons against the clacker of the china plates. Chicken soup, sweet greens with tomatoes the size of peas, rare roast chicken slices, noodles in a red sauce, cheese that melts on your tongue served with the softest bread. My mother was making sure we were keeping our plates full.

"It's good to have you back, Meryl, and most importantly, good to see your mother all happy and about." Mr. Remy was eating slowly, "We are meeting after such a long time, seems like we have a lot to catch up on. So, why don't you tell us what you have been up to? Are you a lawyer?"

"I joined the U.N. after completing my studies and now I am on an assignment in Paris. I didn't want to study law after I left, I made up my mind to join the government services."

"You know, Samantha is engaged, a lovely fellow." My mom could see that we were not talking so she would make sure that we all talked about something, "Why don't you tell Meryl about him?"

"Yes, his name is Jacob, he is a lawyer in my firm," Samantha left her spoon and spoke softly to me, "So everything is not about you."

My mom looked at us realizing the coldness around us.

"No, it's not," I spoke softly, "It's about all of us." I smiled at her.

Samantha rolled her eyes and started eating again. My Mom was insisting on keeping our plates filled. I ate a lot as I was very hungry.

"Why don't you join us tomorrow with your fiancé? I would like to take you both out for a dinner, all four of us and him," I asked Samantha.

"I am a bit busy tomorrow; I don't know if I can make time for that."

"Please, Samantha, let me celebrate a night with you all, for old time's sakes."

"We would love to be there, and I am sure Jacob would love to join us too," Mr. Remy told me. Samantha looked at her dad and said nothing.

After dinner, I helped Mom clean up, she was talking and enjoying every moment of my time with her.

"You told me you wanted to say something to me before going out in the evening. I hope everything is OK," she said, sitting down on the sofa.

I paused a little and then told her, "Yes, I just wanted to tell you that I was doing some voluntary work in Paris but after that, I plan to come here for vacations and whenever I would get time off from my routine."

"Oh my God, that is great news. I am so happy." My mom's eyes were sparkling with bright light, "For a moment though, I thought." She paused and then continued, "I thought that… You know, before you left…and I couldn't tell you something and…I thought you found it out so you left because you were angry…and I thought that…like in the evening, you would tell me why…but it could be a different reason or…" my mom was pressing her fingers.

"Mom, it was nothing," I held her hands in mine, "I left because I was immature, and I wanted to start my own life, but I shouldn't have. I have come to love unconditionally, that is the only form of true love."

"Maybe I owe you an explanation that I should have told you, so the fear of you finding it out –"

"Mom, you don't need to tell me anything and you don't owe me anything. There is nothing in this world that can change my love for you, even if it is knowing that I had been living a lie my whole life. I wouldn't care, Mom. All I am is sorry, and I know I cannot make up for the lost time, but I can be with you for the time to come whenever I can. Unconditional love doesn't demand anything."

My mom looked at me and I felt like maybe she knew that I had learnt it or maybe she didn't, but I didn't want her to feel that she owed me anything. I didn't want her to go through anything else. I just wanted to be there. We sat there quietly while my mom talked about some of the things I used to love as a child.

The next day, I stayed there too, I didn't return to my hotel, and spent it with my mom, I thought I would be staying in the hotel if I couldn't pull the courage to meet her, yet here I was, not wanting to leave her now. We spent the whole day chatting and enjoying and at night, we again got together and met Jacob too. It was a great dinner. We all chatted with Jacob and he told us about how they met.

"Though it's surprising that you guys were inseparable from childhood, but Samantha never mentioned you," Jacob said, smiling, but soon realized that we all got quiet.

"I don't remember a lot of people from my school," Samantha said and excused herself from the table. She went to the terrace that was close to our table. I went up to her and stood by her side.

"He is a great guy," I told her, smiling.

"I know," Samantha gave a short reply.

"I will leave tomorrow, but I plan on coming back after I finish my assignment."

"Sure."

"I told you that I was sorry for what I had done, and I can't undo it, but all I can do is try to make up in the times to come."

"I don't want your sorry, and if it were not for my dad, I wouldn't have come here tonight."

"Then what do you want me to do? I am right here, say anything you want me to hear, and I will take it." I came up close.

"You were always a cold loser, who never realized that I worked hard to stick to you because you were my childhood friend. You found excuses to be mad at others and pity yourself. When you couldn't solve your issues, you came back out of nowhere, expecting everyone to accept you back," Samantha was angry again.

"Are you angry because my parents take me back or that I left you without contacting?" I asked her, but she looked away. "Which ever it is, Samantha, I may have been a cold loser who looked for excuses to stay mad, but I came back, faced everyone, and apologized. And from where I am standing, I see that you are the cold friend who is finding excuses to stay mad at things. I may have let my feelings take the better of me when I was immature, but you are acting like that now. I have burnt in these cold feelings for quite a long time, but I don't want to anymore. And if you don't want anything to do with me, I will not bother you anymore. You can leave the dinner when you like." I left to join my family on the table. Samantha came back after a while and sat down quietly.

"You know, Jacob, Samantha always wished that she had a sister like Meryl," Mr. Remy told us.

"And I remember, they came to me one day, saying that why couldn't they be sisters," my mom laughed with Mr. Remy.

"She was always more than a sister to me and if she would let me be, I would love to be her sister again," I said, looking at Samantha who was looking down.

"You are always my sister," Samantha smiled and there was a feeling of calmness in the air.

A tension that was holding something back at our union seemed to have perished in that one instant. Some issues had seemed to be gone and hurtful emotions had been forgiven. There was an openness and both of our parents were smiling more as we all chatted about the silly things Samantha and I did as children.

The idea that forgiveness is something we do for someone else is the perception of power as the ability to control. The subconscious behind not forgiving is to cause pain in someone, who has hurt us, and thereby alter that person. But the origins of our emotional pain are inside each of us. When we make a choice to not forgive, we inflict pain upon ourselves. Staying angry at others is like trying to cause them pain by banging our head against the wall.

We are the ones who are hurting our own selves when we do not forgive. There is nothing healing, fostering, or even slightly positive about not letting go of issues. If we choose not to let go, then we decide to hold others responsible for our experiences.

We are the sole creators of our own emotions, but the negative feelings experienced by the subconscious hold the others accountable for our response. When we learn to forgive, we stop holding others liable for our emotions. We take the necessary steps to improve our behavior by taking control of our emotions. The blame game is a tool of the ugowens that requires healing, by shifting its energy flow through the consenzis.

We are all imperfect, and at some point or another, we have been hurt by others, just like some of our acts might have offended others. But we can never control how others act or talk, all we can do is decide how we respond. We can either get bothered by it for years, or let it go.

It was a long and pleasant night; we hadn't realized how much time had passed in our joyous conversations. We all bid farewells and though I had to leave early, I felt at no rush.

The next day, my mom was happily making breakfast for me. I thought she would cry a lot before I would leave, but she managed to put on a happy face.

"I am not sad, my dear," she brushed her fingers through my hair, "This is how I always imagined you would leave. A warm goodbye to Samantha and her dad and a brief conversation with me with the promises to meet again."

I touched her scar on the neck, with tearful eyes.

"It was just a small lump, they successfully removed it. It's nothing to worry about, my dear." My mom took my hand and kissed it, "I am very happy that you decided to come. Come to see me whenever you feel like it. This is your home and I will always be waiting for the moment to see you again."

"I am glad that I came too." We hugged and said our goodbyes.

Emre had left for the airport. I quickly took my things from the hotel and checked out to leave. I met Emre at the waiting lounge.

"You feel different," he told me the instant I came close to him.

"I feel different too." I smiled at him.

Chapter 17

It is dark in here once again; I am in the subliminal land, only this time, my feet are not touching the cold floor. I am sitting on a hard chair and there is a table in front of it. I could feel it. I am suddenly blinded by a beam of light that lights up the room. I struggle to open my eyes and rest my arms on the table that is visible to me. I see a man on the other end. He comes forward and I can make out his face a little. I try to figure out his face as he approaches in that light. The blinding yellow light seems to have cast a yellow shade on his face.

I cannot remember being that scared in my life. It is the same face, the same horrifying masked face that I sometimes see in my dreams. I always recall it as the yellow masked stranger. It is him and I cannot believe how yellow his complexion is. It has been vague before but only because my brain always woke me up before such a horrific image covered my mind. And now I am seeing something my eyes will never be able to erase. The absolute horror completely paralyzes my senses, and the more I think about running away, or simply moving a bit, the more I feel discouraged and utterly terrified.

"Don't be scared, nothing can harm you here. I know I appeared in your dreams a couple of times when you were having a hard time letting go of self-seeking thoughts." His forehead is almost square, large, and imposing. A few lines are laid upon it, but they are dismissive as tricks of light. His eyebrows are impossibly straight, his eyes made of rich mahogany. Eyes that express many secrets, but hold them locked in a strongbox so stunning that you wouldn't dare to open in fear of what you might find within. The most striking feature is his pale-yellow complexion. It makes him seem more authoritative than his aura already suggests. It is nothing that he is doing precisely, it just looks as if he has a secret you could enjoy hearing about.

"I see that your acceptance of me has led you to analyze your decisions about your life," he says, leaning forward, "When you become more aware of your life, then the chaos in your subconscious starts to subside. There is more peace."

I am still horrified but try to hide and compose my fears.

"You should know that when you start understanding your ego, then you surely are moving ahead in your life. We here believe that understanding the ego and being able to control is the biggest challenge of all. It is the inner struggle that is the most difficult when you are at war with yourself. You have to take decisions that are not selfish, but the right ones."

I gather the strength to say something, "Are you my ego?"

"I am a part of it. We are never defined by one figure here. Once you start taking control of your feelings, you start watching a voice within yourself, that is your ego. This recognition is the first step towards fulfilling your purpose. It is the first step towards awareness. Most of the humanity stays within these premises. They try to conquer their feelings and start noticing their ego, but that is as far as they can go. Most of the people spend their entire lives living in a chaos of overbearing feelings at unease with a rising ego whose chatter never stops. There are many people who, even at their death beds, curse their enemies and talk about revenge because they have never lived their lives with awareness. They don't know the other sides or levels of awareness.

"In order to achieve the next step, you need to be aware of your ego and then you will enter the next level of wise decisions. That is the level that some of you enter by analyzing your feelings and understanding the voices of your ego. A few of you remain in this phase where you make wise decisions and do better in life than those who stay at the first level. Your decisions at the second level are both based on ugowens and consenzis. You are either making a better decision for yourselves because you want to do good or are scared to lose something but if you continue to stay in this struggle, you pass your entire lives staying here, but if you focus on taking better decisions based on love, then you bring more awareness to your lives. When you learn that the decisions that you make with love and joy are stronger than those based on hate and fear, then you move further to the next level. You achieve the level of conscious ego with the help of love and if you stay with love, then that is the ultimate power of awareness and that means that you have learnt the ultimate truth and achieved your true goal in this life. From that level, everything that you do is a fulfillment of your life's purpose. Every decision that you make is wise and through love, you conquer your ego. If you stay in this level till you die, then you enter the eternal bliss through the power of awareness, not fear."

"So, it is possible to go back a level," I said, still a little scared.

"Yes, always, because your feelings and your thoughts are continuously at play alongside your outer world. The state of awareness is a constant struggle that we have to struggle with. If you lose to the fears, then you go down to being a victim of the voices in your head."

"And we can fight them again too, right?" I interrupt him again.

"Yes, like I said, it's a constant struggle, but once you achieve the level of conscious ego, you get the power to fight your fears in a better way. With every level you are stronger, and your emotions have less control over you, but it doesn't mean that they have perished. Your inner struggle continues as long as you are alive. Your life on this earth is nothing but a test to be more aware and live with consciousness. The power of ultimate awareness is the answer to so many problems that you face in life. It is unfortunate that the number of people who achieve awareness through conscious ego has always been very less, but Wisdom believes that with every passing century, the humans are becoming more and more aware of their choices. They want to live the ultimate life of love and awareness where they are not bound by their ego or controlled by their feelings."

"I think I have defeated my feelings, so you think I have no ego now?" I ask in wonder.

"No one can defeat something entirely; they may seem to go in hiding and if you let loose of yourself again, they will come to haunt you with force. And everyone has ego, even the people who say they have none. You might be able to control or calm it down, but everyone possesses ego. It's a part of who you are. It's not easy to get rid of something that is the defining factor of your personality."

"Why is the ego so strong in defining us?" I ask again.

"The ego creates systems of control in order to keep surviving. These control systems are meant to keep other egos in check, which it can do with some limited success through fear, control, and manipulation. However, these same systems that keep our egos under control, never allow us to thrive as loving beings, because they keep us in a constant state of egotism. Sooner or later, at some point, they become dysfunctional and then through the very same control, they become gigantic, self-centered systems which only serve to grow more and more ego that creates suffering, making more and more people unhappy. These systems include those like religions, media and news, governments, incarceration, financial, political, military, and education systems. People fight over two hundred years' old ideas, making the lives of the living dreadful for the concepts developed by those who have passed away. They define their living conditions by the words of those who had completely different circumstances. The people who are at the top of these egoistic management become consumed with power and the authority that is driven by ego, creates more ego. The ego ends up terminating and consuming itself out of its own egoistic desire to survive. The reason being that we create our own reality and if we are choosing these lower vibration egoistic emotions such as guilt, anger, victimization, control, resentment, jealousy, and fear, at some point, we will also manifest these types of things in our own lives because the universe is a mirror and will give us back from what we put out.

"If someone threatens your social standing, your ego trusts this to be a threat to its survival. If your social standing is reduced, then so is the ability to make money and feed yourselves according to the ego. If someone has a different way of life and belief system, then your ego sees this as a danger. It becomes consumed with trying to change or eliminate the threat. Your ego is threatened by others way of life or identity, presuming that it will overshadow your own. The driving force within the ego is fear and, if you allow it, the ego will install fear into all areas of your life. Any sort of greed, intolerance, and anger are grounded in fear, and ego is watching it all in the background. The ego knows all your weaknesses, your suppressed desires, and it will use them against you, to knock you off your purpose and into the trap of listening to it.

"Ego is an interpretation of realism in which each of us feels isolated from everyone and everything else. Ego creates a division between oneself and others. Everyone is born without a name, but after birth, a person identifies with a name. It's the sight in which each of us positions at the center of the creation and we look out on the whole world and everything in it from our own point of view. We relate to everything in terms of our needs, our understanding, and beliefs. The ugowen ego that is based on fears has a dishonest idea of the world. The real problem with such ego is that it prevents us from knowing ourselves and realizing our own greater potential. This is where your ego serves like a block to your own progress.

"Narcissism and arrogance are what most of us tend to think of when we think of ego, but ego is much more than an overinflated sense of self. It can also turn up in feelings of inferiority or self-contempt because ego is any duplicate you have of yourself that gives you a sense of individuality. That identity derives from the things you have been telling yourself and the things other people have been saying about you that you have come to accept as truth. You stand separate from others based on these self-images and the ego becomes successful in emphasizing the distinctiveness of others.

"This sense of separation is an essential part of the ego. The ego loves to support itself by complaining, either in opinions or feelings, about other people."

The Conscious Ego

"Why do we cling on to ego if it is so damaging to our world?" I ask, as I start to let go of my fear bit by bit now, "Why are we not able to identify it as something negative, like the ugowens?"

"The ego is created for the growth of life from matter. Its distinct obligation is to consolidate actions and suspend harmony, a cautious move, intentionally done in quest of delight. The reason we have ego is because it is necessary for our growth in life. Ego should be there when there is challenge and creativity. The ego is only a blockade to your growth when it is overwhelming and full of emotional misrepresentations and struggles, not otherwise.

"Ego can serve a great purpose. It is the first way we determine a degree of distinctiveness that extricates us from others. However, it is rooted in the unconsciousness that we inherit from our unconscious substantial beginnings. Achieving conscious ego is a powerful struggle. Each time you choose harmony and love in life, you challenge the parts of yourself that want other things. They are the parts of you that are angry, jealous, and frightened. The more you challenge them, the less power they have over you and the more power you have over them. Eventually, their power over you disappears.

"Your challenge will be to become more aligned internally with the truthful reality around you. Fighting with your ego will just make it stronger, as by waging war on it, you make an enemy. By living your potential through a healthy ego, you are in full flow of becoming increasingly self-sufficient. The consenzi ego inspires you to push beyond self-inflicted boundaries and be more personally responsible for your actions, by embracing harmony with others. Confusions, verdicts, blame, or shame are what distort the ego from its consenzi and pure state, into an ego that becomes a transformed ugowen through bottled-up and suppressed anger.

"Bearing a consenzi ego doesn't mean you are giving up any part of yourself. You are only readjusting the part that creates a low energy for you and makes you lose awareness. If you had no ego, you would have no purpose behind living in this world as a unique being. By becoming conscious of the ego, we experience life with awareness and make the choice for peace and love in our lives, rather than suffering.

"There is a way out of this seemly inevitable cycle of egocentricity that traps the entire race, a window of opportunity exists in our lives where we learn to make a choice before this selfishness traps us and we repeat the cycle. It has been prophesied that the burden on every person bearing the ugowen ego will become so great that the collective spirits of beings on the planet will learn to make a united decision that they have had enough experience of the suffering and collective pain. That is when they will choose to experience love from their highest form of awareness and there will be no ugowen left to corrupt their egos. That time might be far, but Wisdom has faith that it will be reached in anyway, because the humans are learning to choose awareness in their search for the eternal truth.

"The frequency of love is not self-consuming, but connecting and evolving. When we live with love, we are recalling the connection that we possess in the material of space-time with all existences across the universe. This united choice is what is called the Conscious Awakening. Everyone has ego and sometimes, we are convinced that if we didn't have it, then the world would be a better place, but that is not true. If everyone was concerned more about everyone and everything else, there would be something lacking in personal individuality. You could be nice without personal growth and purpose. You can never take care of others if you are not taken care of personally."

"So, developing ego into a conscious ego is the final goal. I feel that I am becoming more aware of my own self. I am taking steps to let go of the inner voices," I say with pride because I know that I have learnt to conquer my fears now and I will be on the path to make my decisions through wisdom and love.

"You will do great, but as part of your ego, I am here to help you analyze the decision that you might make in order to fulfill your promise to your grandfather."

"I had forgotten about that for quite some time. I have no intention of moving on with that. I don't want to help in anything that could have a negative impact," I say, trying to cover the topic.

"But your uncle still relies on you for your word and there is a part of you that believed that you needed to do it in the first place," he tells me softly, trying not to scare me again.

"I was angry and sad after my grandfather died, so I thought I would seek my uncle and see how I could take revenge for something that my family had to go through," I am a bit embarrassed, "I don't want to take revenge anymore."

"That's the beauty of life's test, they are so unpredictable and no matter how hard you try, you can never pass them without facing them. You will have to make a wiser decision to undo it."

A man in a long white robe comes and stands next to Ego, "I hope he didn't scare you much."

I nod my head.

"We are all here to guide you, but you are the one who has to make the right decisions. You made a mistake and if you don't want your mistakes to haunt you, then fix them or try to make a decision that doesn't involve abandoning or hurting someone. You know, the best decision for moving in the direction of your purpose is never walking over others for your needs." Lord Wise took out a cube and handed it to me over the table. "Use it wisely. You have done wise in dealing with your emotions and ego. But make sure that you choose with love and do not give into your fears."

I hold the cube and see that it's denser than just a cube. I close my eyes to feel its shape. I open my eyes and find myself in my room with the large red book in my lap and the complex Rubik's cube in my hands.

Chapter 18

"Why did you call me here?" He looked totally different without his church clothes, "We cannot be seen together other than our church unions."

"I had to talk to you," I told him.

"Then we should order something, I will regret never having taken my niece out to lunch," said Akochi, "I am glad that you decided to meet up since our sessions will be ending soon. You are ready for your part for the big day."

"That's what I wanted to talk to you about, Uncle. I don't want to be a part of it anymore," I said, slowly fearing his reaction.

"What? Why would you say that now? When we are so close."

"I am sorry I made a promise to you that I would help you, but I cannot. I have changed and I no longer seek revenge from these people. I don't want my ego to convince me to commit a crime because their forefathers were bound by their egos," I tried to convince him.

"You think you can come to me on the last day before the event and convince me that you will not be a part of this just because you learnt some ego theory." He got angry at me, "I have my deal with you, and you cannot change now." He calmed himself and reminded me of the deal, "Look, my man is going to be in the choir and you have to help him get through security with his white suitcase that will bear a star on it with his name, Eraf, on top of it. You help him do that and he will do his job. But you have to remember to do yours. Don't forget that it's not a promise to me only, but a promise that you made to my father too, who was your grandfather."

"I promised him that I would find you, no matter what it took. I would meet you and bring you back to see your sister. I promised him that I would help his daughter see his long-lost son," I told my uncle, "I never said that I would help you carry out a public execution of a party leader."

My uncle looked shocked and stared at me.

"So, it's true," I said in horror, "I was not going to say anything to you or help you with it before. I was just going to keep my silence, but now I have to do something."

"But you promised me that you could help my guy through security and I told you that if you wanted me to show up to your mom's house, then you would have to help me out with my plan, and where is all this coming from." Akochi was making me feel obligated towards him, "You were the one who was mad at the man who was your father in some way. You were the one who said that your mother and her family suffered as immigrants and you will help our people. You will be able to give peace to your grandfather by helping me against these people who had destroyed the lives of so many immigrants like us."

"I was wrong in thinking that clearing security for your man was a way of helping my own who have always aimed at peace. I was not thinking properly when I shared my anger, but you never clearly told me why you needed me to clear that guy, you just said it was to help our people. I did tell you that I was with you but that never meant that I am against all the innocent people who had no part to play in massacres. I have learnt to make peace with my feelings, and I have changed, Uncle. I made a mistake by being angry before, but that can never justify what your main intention is. You cannot make these people suffer for the mistake of others." I tried to compose myself.

"But I haven't changed, ever since I was little and took refuge in this church, I wanted to take revenge. And I am not about to give up just because my niece had a wake-up call." Uncle Akochi kept his voice low, but he was still angry, "I still remember that day as fresh as it happened yesterday. It was the 17th of October, and my mom had gone out to get something, while Afua and Dad stayed at home. I was a little boy and followed my mom everywhere. We were coming back from the shops when we heard the noise of guns and screams. My dad had told my mom to stay out of it, but she was stubborn at helping her people. I hated what she did. She was so stubborn that I told her I would not stay behind without her. I was always scared of someone taking my mom away from me. I cried and told her not to go but she had to help the drowning child. She told me to stay near the tree and run away if she didn't return. I cried and screamed for her, but she left me because she was sure that she could save the drowning children, or at least help one of them. My mom wanted to help the youngest girl who couldn't breathe in the water. While there was chaos and the sounds of horror, I stood near the tree, crying for my mother in fear. She was pulling the young girl who had been thrown into the water when a policeman came and pushed her in too. She tried to struggle and save the girl, but the police had thrown more people in. It was the most horrible sight of my life that haunts me, but I ran away because I had promised my mom I would. I was very skinny and quick to my pace and ran away, sliding between police lines, where they tried to whip those of our race and said, 'Fellagha, go back to your Ferhat Abbas.' I ran as fast as I could in horror and despair. I escaped so many police lines and came to take refuge in a church where a kind pastor had opened his doors for the likes of us." My uncle paused to hold back his tears, "We wanted to see the leader behind those massacres be punished, but Maurice Papon stayed blessed by the authorities for a long time." Akochi had tears in his eyes but wiped them as soon as he could.

"Actions were taken against Papon. He was tried for his charges and punished too. The French government has always condoned the massacre." I tried to reason with my uncle a little, "Why do you want to execute the present leader of the national front?"

"For years, we waited for this man to pay for his crimes but when he was finally convicted and tried, he died of a heart failure. What a tragedy, when he should have been publicly tortured to death. His attorney declared that Papon should be buried with insignia of Commander of the Legion of Honor. That triggered public expressions of indignation from all French political parties, except the leader of the (Far Right) national front. The Grand Chancellor of the Legion of Honor and politicians strongly opposed this project, but he was still buried with those honors against the wishes of a huge hostile crowd." My uncle was trying to keep his voice low because his anger was getting hard to control for him, "I have worked for years for an opportunity like this one, where we host a seminar with the leader present of the national front as guest of honor. A public execution would help to satisfy the souls of many, as our criminal was buried with honors due to the weakness of such people in government."

"That is not something that you can make these people pay for."

"Maybe not for you, but you don't understand how I feel and how long I have waited for this." My uncle was still angry, "Don't think that you can talk me out of this. I want my revenge in one form or the other and you are going to keep the promise that you kept to your dying grandfather. I will meet your mom after you have helped me to make my plan successful." My uncle told me to eat.

"I just wanted to help you because I was angry at that time and I took a U.N. job to do something for people like me. And when my grandfather passed away and you contacted me, I was thrilled to fulfill my grandpa's promise and bring you back to Mom. I agreed to it, but I had no intention of going on with it later. I was not going to tell anyone about you but now I must set it right and I am asking you not to do it. I believe that it will be a huge mistake and I have done mistakes in my life." I wished that he would understand like I did, "You never realize it at that time when your ego overpowers you, but you always feel bad afterwards." I started eating to make things less suspicious.

My uncle was not ready to listen to any of my reasoning and carried on in a casual tone. Taking something so serious in a casual way was not easy for me because I still got butterflies with fear of what I had gotten myself into. I felt trapped, but I was determined to set my mistake right.

"You will help me do this right thing, yes or no?"

"I will help you do the right thing," I said what I meant.

After I came back from lunch with my uncle, I felt very disturbed, so I sat down, and rested on my couch for a while till I thought of something.

It's so strange that we cannot convince people to understand that they are suffering because of their feelings. I guess they will not accept anything till they have the will to change. The book was right in that; my will to change and achieve consciousness was the first step.

We see the mind like a house, so if your house is on fire, you need to take care of the fire, you do not go to look for the person that set it on fire. Take care of those emotions first; it's the priority. Because anything that comes from a place of fear, anxiety, and anger will only make the fire worse. Calm down, and find a place of tranquil and peace to cool the flame of emotion down.

As a collective energy, fear and anger can be very destructive. We make the wrong decisions if we base it on fear, anger, and wrong perception. Those emotions cloud our mind. We need to feed our minds with awareness to cool down the negative emotions. The old emotional pain living inside of us may have accumulated from past traumatic experiences and sticks around because these painful experiences were not fully faced and accepted, the moment they rose.

By understanding the emotional pain and how to accept our experience in the present moment, we are better able to deal with anger and live a much better life. The reality is that however sweet we may anticipate revenge to taste, we may be in error to expect this. Anger is like taking poison and waiting for the other person to perish. Staying angry is like grasping a hot coal with the intent of throwing it at someone else; you are the one who gets burned. I hold on to the Rubik's cube, I remember playing with it when I was little. My grandfather would help me do it because it was his favorite thing to do when he was alone.

"You need a lot of practice with it, Meryl," he told me, "Make three together here, and let me help you."

"Why didn't you look for your son, Grandpa?" I asked him.

"I did and I even tried going back many times, but your mom and I had managed to escape, and I didn't know how to go back to a place that brought so many horrible memories for us. We started our lives with you here and didn't look back."

My grandpa was showing me how to do the cube, "I tried looking for Akochi through a man I knew in Paris, and after searching for years, he once told me that a man by that name works at some church in Paris who has an African background and lost his parents in the Paris massacre. I didn't try to contact him, but I know it is my son. I always knew he was alive; I just do and if you ever get a chance to meet your uncle, show him this picture of me and his mom holding him when he was little. I am sure he will remember. No child can forget the memories of their parents when they were too little to know anything else."

"Why don't you show him and tell him that you are alive?"

"I would try to, but you see, Meryl, people are always kinder to their next generation and if you go to him with this picture, he will embrace you out of love for his blood but with me, he might still get angry for some reason. People always blame their elders for the miseries that they cannot intercept or somehow find reasons to stay mad at their parents." My grandpa handed me the cube, "Promise me that once you start your job, you will find your uncle and bring him here. I hope you will remember your promise even if I am no longer here. Look here now, this is done."

I solved the cube in my hand like my grandpa used to do it. And when I did, I saw a letter in the middle of each side. O, E, C, I, H, C. I tried to make a word out of these and at last when I wrote it down, it made sense.

Choice; no matter where we are in our lives, we always have a choice to choose which direction we want to go in. In fact, the place where we are in our lives is also a result of the choices that we have been making ever since we can recall. No matter how stuck we feel in our lives, we always have the ability to make a decision in the direction we want to go. The only thing we need to remember is the penalties, for our choices lead us to their consequences and if we manage to analyze the values before making a choice, we become more responsible towards our actions. I have a choice now, just like all those times before this one. I had chosen to seclude myself and then put up with the consequences, then I chose to undo those and made the choice to face the world anyway. I have a choice to do the right thing my own way.

I picked up my coat and left to go to the park. I knew I would find him here, that's where he sits to spend his evening in silence. I saw him on his favorite bench and went up to him. I sat next to him, keeping my calm.

Have you ever looked at the things you do and asked yourself if you are doing this from love, or out of fear? This is the most important question you can ask yourself because it brings you to the most important choice you can make: the choice between love and fear. Not only is this choice possible, it is the choice you were born to make each moment. Choosing to act with love no matter what is happening inside of you and around you, is creating true power. Creating true power depends on your choice. Choosing fear, almost always happens unconsciously. Choosing love, always happens consciously.

"You were doing better when you came back from your home," Emre told me, "Now your feelings seem to be struggling again."

"I have to tell you something but before that, I want you to remember that I am not coming to you as someone who works for you but as the person who came to you for help before. I want you to understand it like a human and help me get my uncle out of it too." I brought the strength to tell Emre about my grandpa's wish and how I came to find my uncle.

"I thought my assignment here could bring me closer to him, yet he made me promise that I would clear a security for one of his guys on the assigned day."

"Why would you agree to the plan on the first place?"

"He said that his guy had a message for the French government, and he couldn't tell me at that time. He said that it was for the good of the people. I told him that I would do anything to help the people who had suffered as immigrants and I was also mad at my own life, so I gave him my word. Now I don't want to do it anymore." I was looking down, "You told us that there was a threat and I confronted him. It's true; his guy brings the message of terror by shooting the national front leader. I am so sorry, but I had no idea what I was getting into. Please help me find a way."

Emre was quiet for some time and kept looking straight.

"Are you mad that I didn't come to you before with this? I should have come forward and let you know but I was stuck with the thoughts in my head and I am trying to handle them as best as I can. I want to help the people, not help others destroy their world."

"I don't get mad, but you have to get your uncle to meet you soon," Emre told me after a while of silence, "Tell him to meet you at the same place for dinner."

"What if he asks me to tell him over the phone whatever it is?" I asked quickly.

"It's not a request. Tell him it's urgent." Emre gets up with me, "Right now. Let's go."

My uncle seemed reluctant on the phone, but I told him it was urgent and necessary if he wanted to do something about the next day.

Chapter 19

"What are you going to do about this?" I asked with nervousness.

"He was a boy who was lost and now plans on taking his anger out some way because he has never been able to do it. People think the best outlet for anger is revenge," Emre told me, "but where there is anger, there is always pain underneath. When we feel ostracized, we're more likely to behave aggressively. Vengeance on those who we think have wronged us can be driven out of a sense of achieving justice and feeling rewarded. Social rejection that makes us feel wounded and unwanted, triggers a need to repair our mood by whatever means available, including through the satisfaction of causing harm to those who have made us suffer. Terrorism can indeed be a viable method of mood repair or self-satisfaction."

"So, will you try to convince him to back out?" I asked, still feeling a bit nervous.

"You can never convince people to understand your logic, unless they find their own awakening. You can't force your opinion when they can't see the light. Order something for all of us," Emre told me, while I looked into the menu, "People have two different sets of systems in their brain for dealing with the world. One is the default system which is activated when not much is happening, and you begin thinking about yourself, and the other is the direct experience network. This is a whole other way of undergoing an experience. When this system is activated, you are not thinking intently about the past or future, other people, or even yourself. Rather, you are experiencing evidence coming into your senses. Like if you are in the shower, you can focus on the warmth of the water hitting your body. Both these systems are contrariwise connected. The more absorbed you are with the indirect, the less likely you will be to think about the direct experience. If you have an upcoming meeting while washing dishes, you are less likely to notice a cut on your hand, because the network involved in direct experience is less active. You don't feel your senses as much. Fortunately, this works both ways. When you intentionally focus your attention on incoming sensory data, such as the feeling of the water on your hands while you wash, it reduces activation of the dialogue circuitry. This is the whole reason we talk about being more aware because we don't want to be lost in the negative thinking of the mind that doesn't help us to lead a better life."

"So, you will offer him something that makes him take his mind off this and at the same time, help him recover his feelings," I asked, feeling a bit relieved.

"We can only try to."

I order some light food as we wait. I saw my uncle quickly making it to my table, he paused a little as he reached our table. He was surprised to see Emre.

"Please sit here," I requested him.

"Why is he here? What is going on?" he asked in a frenzy.

"Please settle down, I just want to help," I helped my uncle settle into the chair.

"I don't believe in playing any games. So, I will be honest that I know about your plans," Emre told him.

"You sold me out. This is how you pay the soul of your grandfather. This is how you turn against your people after promising to help me," my uncle was speaking through his teeth, trying to keep his voice down.

"She didn't do anything, and she doesn't have to. I am the one you will be facing for this now," Emre leaned forward, "I am going to be straight with you. You can either take my offer and let me know by midnight, or wait to be arrested by tomorrow. How many people are involved in this?"

"I am not going to tell you anything."

"Then I guess you can explain it to the CNCIS after you are arrested along with the whole of church staff, including the pastor. He will definitely feel bad for ever having helped innocent immigrants like you." Emre tried to get up.

"They all have nothing to do with it," my uncle said angrily.

"Then who does? Unless you let me know, I will take action by midnight."

"A few years back, I was approached by a man who called me to say that he was my father's friend and wanted to meet me. He showed me some of his pictures with my father and told me that my father had passed away, but he knew about my sister and my niece. He told me that she worked in the U.N. and he wanted me to get her help for clearing a man's security so he can murder the man representing the one party that let the man we all hate, be buried with honor. He worked for the party led by Marco Dejon."

"I thought I found you through the number that my grandfather's friend gave him. He told me his name was Kwame."

"He helped us find each other. Kwame wants me to help this man clear through security for which I needed your help but never told you the real reason. I had to return the favor, but I didn't mind doing it because Papon did not deserve to die with honor and people who honored him do not deserve to live with honor," my uncle was letting out his feelings in anger.

I just realized that being more aware is not difficult but by simply activating your direct experience network by focusing on your senses with a non-judgmental attitude, it can help you engage in the present moment and reduce your anger.

One obstacle to investigating present-centered awareness is the well-established tendency for the mind to wander and become distracted from the present moment, in favor of temporally distant, stimulus-independent thought.

"Marco Dejon is the leader of the terrorist organization that goes by the name LFF (League for freedom fighters). He worked for the NLF, but later on took the victims of the Paris massacre to join his self-made party, LFF. He plans attacks through the victims, but his agenda is larger than just one assassination, the man that you agreed to clear through security will have weapons for others too and it will be a mass-scale assassination for many people there, including your own church. Marco is known for his mass-scale shootings where you can never point out the main reason behind the shooting."

"Are you saying that my father's friend is playing us and having a large-scale shooting to create a terrorist wave in Paris?" Akochi was angry but at the same time, trying to understand what Emre knew.

"I am saying that by midnight, I will have you turn in your father's friend or be prepared for the consequences. I know you are a man of the church and you spend your days helping others, but you still keep your anger against those who caused the Paris attack. It is people like you that these terrorist organizations feed on. Ask Kwame to meet you and message me your rendezvous. The police and the secret services will be there to arrest him." Emre gets up from his chair, "I am sure that after he tells you his real name, you will be more interested in turning him in. Do it soon because I do not intend on explaining myself anymore. You owe it to the people who took you and others like you, when you had nowhere else to go." Emre found his way out.

I left with Emre too. I told him that I would stay with him till I wasn't sure what was going to happen. I was grateful to him for his help. Emre had informed the authorities when we left Akochi. And soon after our meeting, Akochi sent us a message before leaving to meet Kwame.

"If my father, a French aristocrat, fled to Canada for my mom's sake around the eighties, and my uncle was taken up by a church pastor who took pity on him when he was a little boy in the early sixties, then I guess this is not the church we were assigned for," I tried to figure it out while waiting with Emre, "The church that was under 'The Eglise' had been occupied by the sans papiers after the zero immigration policy in the early nineties."

"That's right, Marco was a mature man at that time. Your grandfather might have fled but he was one of those that stayed illegally and is suspected of the civil disobedience strikes ever since," Emre told me, "And if your uncle can help us get to Marco, then that will lead us to the church that these immigrants use as their hideout."

"He must be very old; I mean my grandfather is dead and he was old."

"Could be or could be a young friend of your grandfather's, but we are not sure of his age."

"Do you think Marco will help my uncle?"

"These people who have been deprived of families and homes seek those that could be related to them in some way and Marco cares for your uncle as the son of his lost friend." Emre looked at me and said with a smile, "Don't worry, everything will be fine."

We didn't talk much, but we waited in the park till the man that Emre was in direct contact with, called him to tell us that they got the guy after following my uncle to their meeting place. I was relieved and thanked Emre once again.

"Do you remember that I told you all, that words are our weapon?" Emre smiled at me, "I should be thanking you too, you helped us track down the main guy. Marco Dejon goes by the name of Kwame among his friends."

Chapter 20

Before leaving for home, I came to La Plage de L'Isle-Adam (the Beach of the Island of Adam), which is the largest riverside beach in France. Located about one hour north of Paris by train, this is a little oasis in the small picturesque city of L'Ile-Adam. I wanted to spend my last three days here before leaving. Just by myself, reading my book and living with awareness.

My uncle told me that he would join me on my way back home. He wanted to meet his sister. Oh, I cannot imagine how glad my mom would be.

I went out to enjoy the sandy beach, sitting with my book and stirring the Rubik's cube, I was in a total state of presence, looking at the world around me.

Once we discover that the deepest dimension of who we are, is not our historical or psychological identity but it is the mystery of consciousness itself, then our entire relationship to what it means to be a human being can potentially undergo a radical shift. Instead of being driven through life primarily by the fears, desires, and emotional suffering of a separate ego, we discover a source of motivation for being who we are in this world as loving beings. Our life with all its experiences becomes an uninterrupted flow of opportunities to expand into love, instead of contracting into fear.

We see the power of our choices and the extent of our responsibility for what they create. Chris made a powerful choice to hold together a family that created a responsible love.

When my mom protected me against all the odds and made a powerful choice to care for everyone, that created love for so many.

When Emre chose to overcome his fears, he created a life with a promise to help anyone who struggled with fears.

When my uncle chose to accept those people, who cared for him over his desire for revenge, he helped to put an end to a criminal act of injustice.

When my father chose to take responsibility for his actions instead of running away, he rescued the souls of the abandoned.

When I chose to deal with my feelings instead of pitying myself through life, I became a being with eternal love as a daughter, a friend, a colleague, and a niece. I see that when we deal with love, the experience of love comes to us and passes on to others. Eventually, we learn to generate with love, no matter what circumstances we are in. We learn to see our circumstances differently, too. All of them summon us to love, to deal with love, to allow love.

There is a misconception where people believe that if we were born different or were living under different circumstances, then things would be different. All of our insecurities are based on fear, we cannot improve something that is based on fear. We can try to change circumstances or others but that will never help to improve our lives. When we begin by changing the outside world, we already add to the world that the others are trying to do as well.

The only way to change a life is to start from within, change yourself for the better and the outer world will change itself. A true change for the better comes with feeling love for yourself and then for others. Forgive yourself, improve yourself, and learn to forgive others and give love without fear. If you hate those who hate, you step into the darkness with them, if you have no compassion for those who have no compassion, there is no difference between you and those you complain about. So, the only way to change the world is to change your own energy.

Each human is the carrier of the energy that can bring about a change in this world. If we are blaming the people in our family or the people of the world at large, we need to understand that they have undealt pain within them that is responsible for their negative energy and if I respond with the same kind of unconscious fear, then I am at the same energy with them. I have learnt to challenge that negativity within and embark on the road of awareness.

Whichever energy I possess, I am adding more of that to the world. I choose love and I choose to challenge my fears; I choose to think of others like my own self, struggling through life and I choose to understand what is real. The choices are all mine that determine my own energy.

Chapter 21

I solved the cube again but this time, instead of the six letters I saw many small words on every square, I suddenly realized that I could comprehend the cube moving its side. It was blurry at first and then it became clearer. I could see that its sides were projecting inward and outward. I could see it more clearly; it was actually a tesseract with many squares engraved in it. I could see beyond the real cube, I looked around and felt like the world around me was not flat anymore. My surrounding was zooming in and out like a multi-dimensional environment. I thought I was feeling dizzy, I got up to focus more but I saw a lady in a flowing red dress on a sand-hill towards the direction of the sunset. There was no hill before and how could I see this lady from my vision when I was awake and sitting alone. It was the same lady standing with a black horse who was waiting for me at the top of the mountain. The whole world around me seemed to be filled with rays that zoomed in and out, as I walked towards her.

People believe that they live in a three-dimensional world, covering time in space with matter, but I believe that they are more like two dimensional objects, just confined to matter and space. At a few times, they end up being confined to one dimension where they see and analyze their world from only one perspective of matter. Things exist for them as matters and they remain stuck in life with their long-held beliefs that have been passed onto them from generations. They live for these beliefs and die fighting with people for those beliefs, without having ever analyzed them in anyway.

A square is reduced to a line between two dots by these people. They neglect to see the three-dimensional reality of this world; it is just a sliced picture of a square, not the reality of the cube. The world has so much more to offer us, we claim to see the three-dimensional, yet most people don't even see that.

How could they even understand a four-dimensional perspective when they all fail to see beyond the one dimension of material objects? I feel like I am a multi-dimensional object passing through this three-dimensional perceived reality of this world. Our world could be three, but our lives are multi-dimensional in the sense that they stretch back in time to our birth and forward to our death. Each moment is a slice of these four-dimensional objects. Every moment bears a magnitude of other dimensions that create the energy that is not visible to the normal human experience of three-dimensions. The energy of the universe exists through infinite dimensions. The human experience goes up to only fourth of those dimensions that is engraved in the subconscious mind.

My consciousness is a link to my existence in many more dimensions. My existence is a result of a multidimensional presence which I was observing in four dimensions. My experience was flat to the purpose of my life when I did not focus on the energy that I possessed. Our worlds cannot be experienced as three-dimensional, unless they extend for a certain period of length in time that serves as fourth dimension to the living experience of life. When time ceases to exist for one material person, then the person ceases to exist. One dimension requires a support of the other to sustain life. Similarly, time cannot exist without matter. For there to be time, there has to be movement of some three-dimensional object. Our three-dimensional universe is curved in the fourth dimension of time to provide a living experience. My life experiences are a product of time, where each one is different from the previous one. Moving through three dimensions as a result of gaining time, I also possessed energy that supported me throughout my experiences. What I was aware of in this four-dimensional space-time continuum was only a small part of the reality of my existence.

The dimensions beyond time are composed of these energies which are infinite. The energy within is stored as part of the mass possessed by us in the form of feelings. I understand what the book has been trying to tell me, now as I walk in a five-dimensional universe, where my consenzis provide me the strength to move higher. The higher our energy, the more dimensions we experience.

I could see more clearly as I walked towards the horse, the lady in red robe was the most beautiful woman that I have ever seen or heard of. She was the image of the true definition of Love that was in the red book. She was love itself, waiting for me to come closer. She stood there in her magnificence as I walked through five or more dimensions, feeling the higher forms of energy.

My path towards love had always been straight but I chose to be distracted before and now, I choose wisdom and higher energy so that I can reach love, the power of ultimate awareness. I choose to live with love everyday so I can reach the ultimate level of awareness. The distractions in my way had been the chaos of everyday life but awareness is the straight path that helps me to ignore these disorders in life. I can be in two places by covering time, I can be in one place at one time, at another in a different time but I am moving through both space and time now, through a fifth dimension. The only thing that can help me achieve this is my conscious energy, for it is through my subconscious that I have been able to travel backwards and forwards in time. I have used my thoughts to relive the past and now I use my consciousness to achieve my goals and move forward in life. Our consciousness and subconsciousness exist in a dimension beyond the fourth or more. Therefore, my mind and body have been in a paradox because my mind doesn't exist in the three-dimension, like my body.

The time is different from the other physical dimensions, yet consciousness is different to all these dimensions. My mind had enabled the fifth dimensional reality to manifest in our four-dimensional universe. Thoughts are the creation of a world in our minds, that have time and space components to them, imprinted in our subconsciousness, that hold the feelings within its realms. These feelings that give rise to negative or positive emotions help to create energy. The higher the energy, the more consciousness we gain, which is outside of time and space. Awareness is not the same as thinking or feelings, it is the effect of a higher form of energy, created through organized decisions based on wisdom.

My journey through the book helped me to choose with love and wisdom to acquire a conscious ego that has helped me walk through this fifth dimension. We came from beyond this four-dimensional universe and one day, I will go to a universe that is beyond our comprehension as four-dimensional beings.

The ultimate truth of this world is to move from the fourth dimension to the state of being outside of dimensions; a uniqueness, the point from which other dimensions are made of. This, I feel is consciousness and reaching here makes me feel free, not only in space and time, but beyond the four dimensions that I was aware of. I reach love and find love with passion in my heart and a will to improve myself and the world around me. I embrace this reality of life and realize that each one of us possesses this cosmic process. We are always adding energy into this world through our emotions and our actions.

I look at love and I feel enchanted by its grace. She smiles and hands me the reins of the horse. I smile at love and what I see is my own reflection, I see me, I see you, I see us, all radiating the energy of love and consciousness.

It is not the quantity of energy but the type of energy that we add in order to make a difference in this world. No matter where you are or what you are doing, you are creating a difference in this world with your energy.

Feelings, thoughts, and emotions play a vital role while physics helps us see the significance of how we all feel. If all of us are in a peaceful loving state inside, it will no doubt impact the external world around us and influence how others feel as well. So, what really matters is not when you do things, but how you do everything in your life, with every passing minute.

The color of love flows through our veins with purity, unless we choose to poison it with fear, the choice lies within each of us.